your pastor's heart

your pastor's heart

Serving the One
Who Serves You

E. Glenn Wagner
&
Glen S. Martin

MOODY PRESS
CHICAGO

ISBN: 0-8024-3387-1

1 3 5 7 9 10 8 6 4 2

Printed in the United States of America

To all the pastors who,
by serving the Lord Jesus,
have accepted the highest calling of all,
to "shepherd the flock of God."
To your shepherd's heart we dedicate this book.

contents

	Foreword	9
	Acknowledgments	11
	Preface	13
1.	The State of the Pastorate	15
2.	Great Expectations	25
3.	Exposing Myths in the Pastorate	33
4.	The Pastor's Role	45
5.	Preyed on or Prayed for	57
6.	The *M&Ms* of Support	75
7.	Positive Participation	87
8.	Biblical Teamwork	101
9.	Following the Leader	119
10.	Seven Qualities of an Effective Church	133
11.	Pastoral Temptations	147
12.	How to Support Your Pastor	167
	Notes	183

HEARTBEATS

The following exercises and charts offer ways to better know your pastor's heart as well as your own. They also will help you improve your heart as a servant and give many suggestions for encouraging your pastor.

1. Measuring Your RQ (Responsibility Quotient)   26
2. Checklist for Spiritual Gifts and Natural Abilities   80
3. How to Hear a Sermon   93
4. Dynamic Team Assessment   110
5. Seven Ways to Strengthen Your Pastor's Heart   116
6. Attributes of a Godly Follower   123
7. How Am I Doing As a Follower?   130

foreword

Research at Promise Keepers has identified that pastors need support beyond what they currently experience. To truly be a Promise Keeper is to recognize it is not only a responsibility but a biblical mandate to support and encourage the local shepherd, the pastor of your church.

Most pastors we have met have longed to become men after God's own heart, just as David was. In *Your Pastor's Heart,* Glenn Wagner and Glen Martin show you how to know and strengthen your pastor's heart. They have put together a comprehensive look at a crucial need in our country: how to rightly support our pastors.

In stadium after stadium across America as we have called for pastors to come down front before the platform to receive the prayers of the men in the stands, their hearts have been touched by the affirmation they receive. I will never forget the tears. I will never forget the cheers.

In the following pages you will see a vision for significant encouragement to our pastors. You will learn how pastors feel and the many responsibilities they carry, which can often be overwhelming. But above all you will find practical ways to come alongside your pastor to help and encourage him. I pray that as you read this book you will catch the vision to strengthen the heart of your pastor, the one God has called to shepherd and lead His people.

BILL MCCARTNEY
FOUNDER, PROMISE KEEPERS

acknowledgments

This book has come into existence thanks to the input and assistance of some very special people. We especially want to thank our good friend Dale Schlafer, vice president of Promise Keepers. His heart for pastors has stirred us on to love and good deeds.

Our thanks also to Jim Bell, editorial director of Moody Press, who followed up on our desires and encouraged us throughout the process of writing this book.

To Dian Ginter, thank you for the many hours of editing and for smoothing the rough edges of our words. A special thanks is due Jim Vincent, who (with great gentleness) did the final editing of the manuscript on behalf of Moody Press.

We also desire to express our gratitude to our own flocks that we have the privilege of serving, Calvary Church of Charlotte, North Carolina, and Community Baptist Church of Manhattan Beach, California. The members of both churches have set examples of how pastors can be cared for in a God-honoring way. Thank you for knowing and caring about our hearts.

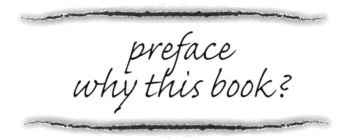

preface
why this book?

We had never met before. We had arrived at the airport from different parts of the country and were trying to find the van and driver who was to take us to the graduate school where we would be teaching a doctrinal course.

As we piled into the very back of the van, we went through the normal pleasantries and found out that not only were we both pastors, but we were a part of the same association of churches. From there our conversation intensified. To this day we don't know whether the trip that should have been a mere thirty minutes took an hour and a half because of God's intervention or simply due to a driver with memory (or directional) loss. But during that ride of conversation and growing nausea (backseat, mountain roads), a friendship was born.

In that first of many conversations, Glen and I discussed our call to ministry, the trials that pastors face, and our deep love for the church and her shepherds.

Please hear us. We don't just like the church and her pastors, we love them. As a result, we both give a significant portion of our time to training, equipping, and encouraging pastors. And that's the reason for this book. We know that most church folks love their pastors, but don't always know how to show it and are often unaware of the unique pressures that pastors face.

It is our prayer that this book will encourage you to help your pastor become the best pastor you've ever had.

Each of us has met with pastors and church leaders through the years in our roles as seminar leaders and speakers, educators and students, and conference attendees and pastors who have reared their families in largely supportive congregations. Glenn has served as vice president of ministry advancement for Promise Keepers and continues to speak and write on issues of pastoral ministry, mentoring, and men's ministry. Glen has served as a pastor in several medium to large churches, and consults with churches on leadership, small groups, and evangelism issues. In our travels and counseling we have met pastors who have experienced pressures and misunderstanding, and congregations with both loving and insensitive members. This book is intended to help you understand and encourage your pastor's heart.

We will offer plenty of ideas along the way for supporting your pastor. But the basic strategy is actually an attitude. Pastor David Fisher has summarized it well. As he explains:

> I was talking to a lay leader in a great church not long ago. He asked how I was doing and then said that he was worried about his pastor. We had a few minutes of truth telling about the difficulties of church leadership, especially the loneliness of it.
>
> Finally, he said, "What can we do for you guys, anyway?" I was taken by surprise—as no one had ever asked me that. "Just love us," I said. In all the expectations, demands, and pressures of church life, love is what seems to be lacking. Ironic, isn't it, given the nature of the gospel?[1]

We desire that you become someone who shows greater love for your pastor. When you do, you will find it a rewarding experience to work with God's undershepherd for your church and to minister hand in hand to accomplish all God desires to do through your church. When we do this, our churches can be places that show to the world our unity and the love of God; they will be radiant lights in our communities.

1

the state of
the pastorate

Every year the president of the United States travels to Capitol Hill to report on the state of the nation as he sees it. His State of the Union message, delivered to the U. S. Congress and a national television audience, reviews progress in the past twelve months and looks ahead. His report, required by law, includes a detailed plan on how to address the problems and face the new challenges he has identified for the coming year. Senators and congressmen from both sides of the aisle applaud frequently; for that night, at least, there is a sense of unity and goodwill; our problems are less apparent.

It is wise for our nation to pause and look at where we are. As Christians, we need to do the same thing if we are to maintain our cutting edge and accomplish all God has asked us to do. What is our spiritual condition, especially with those who lead us? What is the State of the Pastorate?

The report is not all positive, but like the president's message, the authors will declare positive ways to address the problems and face the challenges. You and fellow members of your church can comfort and strengthen your pastor's heart.

We must first report on the heartache. As much as we travel, we are no longer surprised by the number of pastors we meet who are ready to throw in the towel. Gordon MacDonald wrote several years ago, "Statistics suggest that about one-third of all pastors do ponder the implications of leaving what they thought might be a life work. That figure seems fairly consistent with the overall attrition rate of men and women who have entered the ministry and sooner or later have left it for something else in the non-religious sector."[1]

Those numbers have grown in recent years. In a major survey in the early 1990s, 40 percent of 5,000 pastors reported they had considered leaving the ministry within the prior three months. Looking at that finding, H. B. London, vice president of ministry outreach at Focus on the Family, explained: "Pastors feel victimized because the work is harder and more complicated than ever before. They work harder now and see less response and few results."[2]

A REPORT FROM THE FRONT

The pressures pastors face are diverse. Pastor Steve Roll has written a powerful description of some of the tensions ministers encounter while leading their flocks. In *Holy Burnout* he reviewed his first five years as a pastor. He began excited about his first pastorate. His relationship with the congregation was wonderful: sweet notes, long letters of encouragement, and words of praise. His ministry took off like a rocket, the church was growing, on fire and alive! He was full of enthusiasm and vision; with God he felt invincible. He was certain nothing could stop their church from having a great impact for the Lord.

But then things started to change.

"Something happened on the way to the Promised Land. In the midst of growth and victories, Satan launched a vicious attack against my leadership. Success came to a screeching halt."[3]

He explained how pastors face spiritual warfare and should expect it, because they are fighting for men's souls.

> Conflict with the world is predictable and inevitable if you're trying to do anything important for the Kingdom of God. . . . I was, however, ill-prepared for the fierce opposition that arose from within the four walls of God's house. Satan's strategy was simple: divide and conquer. The enemy was very smooth and subtle in the beginning. Little

things popped up. Personality conflicts. Differences of opinion. Style preferences. Rumblings through the church grapevine questioning my decisions.

Petty matters took center stage. [Roll then listed several, concerning bulletin changes, carpeting, paint color, etc.] . . . Changes that came with growth rocked the boat. The status quo had been turned upside down. New ways threatened the "we never did it that way before" mindset. As the new pastor, I became the target of attack because I was the chief boat-rocker.[4]

From there it was "open season" on the pastor, according to Pastor Roll. He began receiving nasty letters and discovered hidden agendas at board meetings. He recounted the wounds that Satan inflicted through the sheep, the power plays, the politics. "The gossip holes were well-watered by self-appointed watchdogs who believed it was their religious duty to keep the pastor in line. My authority was challenged. My motives became suspect. My character riddled by innuendo and misjudgment of my heart."[5] Divisions came and finally splits occurred as the well-intentioned and the downright manipulative and/or vicious wolves in sheep clothing tore apart the unity of the church. Finally the pastor was asked to leave, as the powerful members were able to impose their desires on the weaker faction that was backing the pastor.

It is heartrending to read how this once confident, enthusiastic, vibrant man was almost destroyed by those to whom God had called him. At one point, wrote Roll,

> The war in our church produced countless casualties. I can only speak for this wounded warrior. Criticism cut my heart. Misunderstanding of my motives stung my spirit and slashed my self-confidence. Attacks on my character sliced gaping wounds in my self-esteem.
>
> I felt like a person who had been jumped and stabbed repeatedly. With each wound, I bled emotionally. Cut, bleed. Slash, bleed . . . the wounds got bigger and deeper. They bled profusely.
>
> After five years of unceasing conflict, my emotional tank rested on E. Leaving under pressure was the final blow that drained the last fumes of emotion and sucked the spiritual life out of my soul.[6]

Like Pastor Roll, many a pastor can identify with David in Psalm 55:12–14 when he says, "If an enemy were insulting me, I could endure it; if a foe were raising himself against me, I could hide from him. But it is you, a man like myself, my companion, my close friend, with whom I once enjoyed sweet fellowship as we walked with the throng at the house of God."

One denominational study of 276 active and 241 former pastors attempted to discover why pastors are burning out and subsequently leaving the ministry. Researcher Andre Bustanoby identified three specific areas generating most of the pain and heartache in the pastorate.

> 1. Conflict with the congregation (such as unwarranted criticism), too high an expectation for the minister and family in their personal lives, apathy and lack of cooperation on the part of the church leaders;
> 2. Distortion of the role of pastor (too much time spent in administration and in smoothing the easily ruffled feathers of the church members, too little time for study and personal contact);
> . 3. Personal problems (such as a sense of personal and professional inadequacy, insufficient training, family problems).[7]

CAUSES OF PRESSURES ON OUR PASTORS

These may be the symptoms, but there still remains the underlying causes for these kinds of pressures on the pastor. We have seen three predominant sources for this stress and lessened commitment in the pastorate.

Spiritual

First, there is a spiritual reason. Don't be surprised when we tell you that Satan has targeted the pastor of your church. Despite what you may have thought, the real battle is not between the pew and the pulpit, the real battle is "against the rulers, against the authorities, against the powers of this dark world and against the spiritual forces of evil in the heavenly realms" (Ephesians 6:12b). Satan does not want your pastor to be successful in reaching people for Jesus Christ. Satan will do everything he can to disrupt the work of God in your church, even if that means destroying the family and integrity of your shepherd.

After all, why not? If the shepherd is brought down, the sheep will inevitably suffer. London and Wiseman put it succinctly: "When pastors are at risk, the church of Jesus Christ is also at risk."[8]

Not only will the involved church be affected, but with today's modern means of communication and the desire of many media leaders to point out flaws in Christianity, the impact of one man's fall can touch the lives of many outside his normal sphere of influence.

Look at the way the media thrived on the scandals of the "men of the cloth" in the late 1980s and early 1990s. Those fallen Christian leaders simply added fuel for those already wanting to destroy people's confidence in Christianity. The mass media tend to target born-again believers or those the media believe they can link in a negative way to Christianity, such as the cultists. The David Koreshes and Jim Joneses of the world become the standard image of Christianity the media choose to portray as typical. More and more the mainstream media is painting believers as untrustworthy, unstable simpletons who are dangerous to our American society. Such terms as "radical right" and "extreme Christian right" find their way into the nation's newspapers and over its airwaves.

This is not a humanly organized attack, but rather a spiritual one. We are convinced that Satan, the enemy of our souls, is strongly influencing and orchestrating such attacks. The church is one of his main targets, with the pastor being the lightning rod.

So in keeping with his desire to undermine your pastor, Satan has tried to disparage all Christian leaders. A kind of guilt by association. The more he can pull down, the greater impact he has on the good leaders. The more he can attack the authority and reputation of pastors, the more he is apt to weaken the trust of the sheep in any shepherd. This allows the door of suspicion to be opened to this "accuser of our brethren" (Revelation 12:10 KJV).

Such reports of pastoral failure encourage sheep to operate outside the scope of biblical guidelines given to run the church. These attacks by the enemy result in human reasoning being used instead of godly principles. Too often we see sheep trying to lead, dictating to the pastor how they feel God wants him to lead the sheep, when they should be following the shepherd, who is in turn following God's leading. Such wrong practice can also lead to sheep trying to usurp the role of the shepherd, all done in the name of being theologically pure. Too often the God-given authority of the pastor is either watered down or completely undermined by those who try to lead the pastor in their own ways.

God does not change. He is a God of order. When He sets up a pattern, He does not go back and make changes and adjustments simply because that is what people want. Whenever we see God letting man make changes, there is always a price to be paid, whether it's the individual or the church that departs from God's perfect pattern. Is this not what is being written to the seven churches mentioned in Revelation 2 and 3? In each case, the members had strayed to some degree from God's pattern and needed course corrections. Thus we need a person—a pastor—who can assume the responsibility for initiating such changes when the Lord shows him to do so. There has to be that final authority if things are to run smoothly. (We will discuss the pastor's proper, biblical role in chapter 4.)

Emotional

Second, there is an emotional reason for the decline in pastors' commitment to the pastorate. By emotional, we mean the slippery slope of burnout in the ministry. The causes range from feelings of fear, hurt, and alienation, triggered by such things as criticism, false rumors, and pressures to please people. Many pastors simply reach the point where they can no longer go on; they run out of fuel and fail to find the necessary reserves to draw from.

One pastor once told us, "I feel like I am at any given time a week away from total collapse." With this kind of internal exasperation, how can we expect from the pastor the kind of spiritual fervor needed to lead a church and minister to a hurting congregation?

Pastor David Fisher puts it succinctly:

Ministry just plain hurts most of the time. I weary of rumors and of unrelenting criticism by people who should know better. I'm tired of blame and misplaced anger. I wonder if anyone hears and obeys the Word of God. I have spent more hours in nonproductive board and

20

committee meetings than I can count. I am all too aware that I am not fit for this work; and I'm tired of people telling me that or implying it. The truth hurts. I want to quit more often than I want to admit. With Paul I cry, "Who is equal to such a task?"[9]

Another source of emotional stress is the type that Pastor Roll experienced—opposition. It takes a high toll on a pastor's energies and enthusiasm. Unjust criticism can be used by Satan against a pastor with the same effect as a needle piercing a balloon. Both can deflate, wound, or even destroy.

Still another type of emotional stress comes when the pastor faces pressures to minister in a different way than he has been trained. The fast-changing, often unusual mixture of age groupings found in the church of the 1990s often creates hidden stresses. Authors John and Sylvia Ronsvalle offer one example of those hidden stresses:

> Pastors are feeling pressured to offer more specialized services as they compete to attract new (or transferred) members. As one pastor described his embracing a people-pleasing approach to ministry, "We don't feel we have any choice." A different pastor described the situation saying, "Jesus played with the children and taught the adults. We teach the children and let the adults play."[10]

Physical

The emotional pressures are often intertwined with the third cause of pastoral pressures, the physical. From a physical standpoint, long hours are standard for almost all pastors. For them it is not a cliché—there really are not enough hours in the day to do all they want to do, let alone all that others expect of them. They valiantly try, but too often they end up hurting themselves emotionally, as we have seen, and also physically from not taking proper care of their bodies. They miss meals, eat poorly as they grab something on the run, and don't have (or take) the time to get enough exercise. Many ministers don't get enough rest, and often when they do, the crises of the day and in people's lives weigh so heavily upon them that they don't rest well. There are also the recurring phone calls in the middle of the night to meet some emergency. Such calls not only interrupt badly needed rest, but can have an emotional toll as a weary pastor dreads the ring of the phone.

As pastors we know the feeling of not looking forward to Thanksgiving and Christmas. We love the season, of course, but anxiously await the crises in family lives, which increase along with the pressures of the holidays. For some, the crises come from being alone; for others, they may arise from a lack of money. It does not matter; our phones ring and knocks on the door come more frequently; and we are counseling more. Happy holidays for most end up being times of greater stress and strain on the average pastor. The accompanying guilt of not looking forward to what should be a wonderful time of the year adds to the physical and emotional symptoms pastors can have.

RAISING TIRED ARMS

Though the pressures pastors face are great, the resources God provides are too. And one of the greatest resources is God's people. *You can encourage your pastor's heart.* That is the focus of this book. To understand how you and fellow members of your church can step in to help the pastor bear the great burden he carries, let's look at a powerful example in Moses' time.

It was a time of war for Israel, just as we Christians have wars today with the enemy of our souls. But in this ancient war, the enemy was easy to spot. Exodus 17 tells us that the Amalekites were on the attack. Joshua was in the thick of the battle, with Moses standing on the top of the hill holding up the staff of God in his hands. As long as his hands were raised, Joshua and his men were winning. But have you ever tried to raise your hands over your head for any period of time and just hold them there, let alone have something in them? The strongest of men will eventually have to lower their hands. That's what happened to Moses; his muscles would fatigue and his arms would droop. In this case, there was an unseen spiritual element as part of this picture. Whenever Moses' hands lowered from fatigue, Joshua started losing immediately.

It didn't take long for two of Moses' disciples—Aaron and Hur —to see what was happening. They stepped in, one on either side of their shepherd-leader, and held up his hands so the battle could be won. Without them there would have been a disaster engulfing the Israelite family. The enemy would have been able to defeat them, plunder and enslave them. But because two men came alongside their leader to help him do his God-given task, victory was secured where defeat had seemed inevitable.

Our situation is no different today. The enemy is at the door of the members of our congregation. Our pastor-shepherd has a role to play in helping his people win their battles. He doesn't physically fight the battle, but he definitely plays a key role in helping each of us be victorious. But as with Moses, he can't do his job alone. It takes others to come alongside of him. Now remember, no matter how skilled Aaron and Hur may have been, what they needed to do in this situation took no great training or brains—just their availability to be used to hold up the hands of their leader.

God has not changed His method of operation even today. He allows each of us to be part of winning the battles the body of Christ faces. This may not always be on the front line as Joshua and his men were, nor may it even be in a visible place as Moses was. But it may be in a seemingly insignificant role of holding up one arm of a key person. Authors John and Sylvia Ronsvalle summarize the concept:

> For the contemporary church, the mandate is for lay leaders to help pastors by coming alongside them and their families to facilitate their time, finances, and lives. Like Moses, they need someone to hold up their hands in battle and to perform lesser duties so they can give themselves to eternal kingdom concerns. Ministers need someone to free them from minutia so they can do what God called them to do. Ministers need someone to befriend them, to care for them, and to lovingly keep them accountable for essentials.[11]

There are many ways we can lift up our pastor's arm; we will look at several shortly. One very important part of holding up the hands of your pastor is to pray regularly and strategically for him. In chapter 5 we will look in depth at how to pray and provide an invaluable prayer shield to protect your pastor in all he does.

To lift our pastor's arms—and encourage his heart—we must be ready to assist. But something gets in our way—something called the responsibility quotient, or RQ. To learn more about RQ and to measure your own RQ, read the next chapter.

2

great expectations

In a country where beauty and brains are applauded and intelligence can bring big bucks as a computer programmer or rocket scientist, most people have heard of the test measuring their IQ, or intelligence quotient. An average level of intelligence is 100; those scoring 140 or above (on a scale of 200) are considered intellectually gifted. Most church attendees are well aware of their own intellectual capacity, and some may have even taken an IQ test. But how many true devotees of the Lord's church have ever measured their own RQ, or responsibility quotient? The responsibility quotient reveals the extent of one's expectations of a pastor.

Many of us have great, lengthy expectations when it comes to the tasks and skills needed for a pastor. When we determine our own RQ, we begin to recognize the extent and reasonableness of those expectations.

TESTING YOUR RQ

The following listing of responsibilities and activities is part of the regular work-month of a pastor, whether he serves in an urban, suburban, or rural church. We recognize that depending on the size of the congregation, not every one of the following may be "on the plate" of every pastor. In some cases church committees will have sole responsibility or share with the pastor in some of these items. Yet the vast majority of the duties on this list fall to the pastor—or congregational members expect them to fall to the pastor.

Complete the RQ test that begins below. Take some time to place the number of hours each week you feel your pastor should be focusing on each of the areas. Make sure you take into account the number of hours involved in driving or walking from one place to another as you consider each of these areas.

HEARTBEATS

MEASURING YOUR RQ (RESPONSIBILITY QUOTIENT)

_____ Personal study for spiritual growth and intellectual stimulation

_____ Sermon preparation (include Sunday P.M., any midweek service)

_____ Worship service preparation (choosing hymns/songs, order of service, etc.)

_____ Teaching new members classes

_____ Teaching baptism classes

_____ Visiting members who have become inactive

_____ Solving problems in the church school

_____ Working with school leadership

_____ Visiting shut-ins and the elderly

_____ Hospital visitation

_____ Visiting and evangelizing the new visitors from the weekend services

_____ Caring for the bereaved and planning/leading funerals

_____ Regular visitation to stay up-to-date on regular attendees

_____ Counseling families and marriages in crisis

_____ Emergency counseling: runaways, the depressed, suicidal, abused, etc.

_____ Mediating church and leadership conflicts/disagreements

_____ 24-hour emergencies: illness, catastrophe, accidents, etc.

_____ Fire fighting: solving disputes between the committed membership

_____ Attending committee meetings: missions, C. E., trustees, building, etc.

_____ Attending leadership board meetings

_____ Attending church functions

_____ Attending class socials and parties

_____ Preparing for staff meetings

_____ Staff meetings

_____ Speaking opportunities outside the church

_____ Community involvement; maintaining contact with the lost

_____ Premarital counseling

_____ Conducting weddings (including rehearsal and attending rehearsal dinner)

_____ Denominational involvement

_____ Meeting with missionaries (departing and returning missionaries)

_____ Serving on boards and committees outside the church to promote Christian colleges, seminaries, and camps

_____ Attending various conferences for continuing education and motivation

_____ Administrating the entire church and being available if needed at all activities

_____ Being responsible for all financial activities and promotion

_____ Budgeting procedures

_____ Personal correspondence for encouragement and support

_____ Answering phone calls

_____ Answering correspondence, including e-mail

_____ Talking to people who only "need a minute"

_____ Training future leaders

_____ Planning special events: retreats, camps, parties, appreciation dinners

_____ Writing personal cards of congratulations to members on birthdays and anniversaries

_____ Recruiting help for the nursery, toddlers, and primary departments

_____ Teaching Sunday school (all preparation time)

_____ Writing articles for the church's bulletin and newsletter

_____ Keeping up to date by reading books, articles, and journals

_____ Leading, teaching, and promoting Vacation Bible School or Back
Yard Clubs

_____ Going to ministers' breakfasts, prayer meetings, and other outside functions to retain clergy contacts and support

_____ Actively involved in small groups and the training of small
group leaders

_____ Maintenance around the church

_____ Dealing with city and government officials, such as fire and
safety inspectors

_____ Opening and closing of facilities

_____ Sleeping

_____ Meals

_____ Recreation

_____ Family time

_____ Time alone

_____ Total RQ

_____

We may have forgotten a few items of responsibility. But if you belong to the company of the "typical church member," you have probably gone back two or three times to adjust times, readjust priorities, and then one last time readjust the schedule, recognizing that at any moment an emergency may walk into the office of the one whose day you have orchestrated right down to a working lunch and a long ministry evening out.

What was your total? It shouldn't exceed 168 hours, since that is the total available in seven twenty-four hour days. Now go back and subtract the hours for sleeping, meals, recreation, family time, and time alone. Assuming your pastor receives at least one day off each week, seven hours of sleep and one and one-half hours eating daily, and a weekly minimum of eighteen hours for recreation, family time, and time alone, your RQ score should be 75 or less. Did you exceed that?

Are you beginning to see your pastor's dilemma? Many written and unwritten expectations crowd in on his schedule, and the tyranny of the urgent becomes the rule of the day. No wonder the pastor has tired arms. Add to these expectations being on-call twenty-four hours a day, normally taking only one day off each week (which too often gets interrupted with an "emergency" or "urgent" need), limiting vacation time around the calendar of the church, and a sense of fear about taking more than two weeks off at any given time; and you have the lifestyle of some of the most devoted and tired servants on this planet!

Most pastors resemble the plate jugglers on the old *Ed Sullivan Show.* The more plates kept in the air, the more positive feedback they receive. So, they become trapped into thinking that if they remain "in Christ" and are constantly "in church," then they must be "invaluable." The tragedy that naturally follows if not corrected is that the pastor remains "in Christ" and "in church," but now finds himself "in crisis." Who will lift those tired arms?

A CONGREGATION THAT HELPS

The answer should be obvious—the members of the church. Look back for a minute at the RQ list. Are there not a number of things on that list that the congregation really should be doing for their busy pastor? (Mark them with an "L" for laity.) Things like maintenance, teaching a Sunday school class, and even keeping tabs on those who have gone away to college. Yes, he can do all these things, but the question is, "Will he be able to do *everything* and do it all *well?*" Or will he have to do only an adequate job on some of the items or skip them completely because of time constraints? Or will his health and energy level, even his emotional well-being be affected by the overload of work expectations? And then will some of the members become upset because he is not doing everything they want him to do in the way they want? Remember Pastor Roll?

This RQ list clearly shows how the good can be the enemy of the best. It is a list full of good, better, and best things to do. The disciples in the first century ran up against the same mountain of expectations. They found that they were doing many good things that interfered with their true call, the best. This is why they decided, "'It would not be right for us to neglect the ministry of the word of God in order to wait on tables. Brothers, choose seven men from among you who are known to be full of the Spirit and wisdom. We will turn this responsibility over to them and will give our attention to prayer and the ministry of the word'" (Acts 6:2–4).

The church for many years followed this pattern. But it seems that in the twentieth century, with all the emphasis on self and what makes me feel good, the pastor has once again become overburdened with doing too much. He is no longer viewed as the shepherd, who exists to mobilize and to lead, but is considered an employee, hired by the church to fulfill everyone's expectations and needs.

A couple years ago at a seminar we were teaching in Georgia, we met a pastor who described how a group of people from his church came to visit him. After the pastor and the people exchanged pleasantries, the group members began to voice their concerns about the direction of the church and his overall ministry. When he tried to explain that this was the direction that he believed God had led him to, they remarked: "But you work for us."

That is part of myth one, which we will look at in depth in the next chapter. In fact, this self-centered lifestyle of today's world has exacerbated the problem. Is this part of what Paul is expressing in

Philippians 2:21, "For everyone looks out for his own interests, not those of Jesus Christ"?

Through the years, church researcher George Barna has inter-viewed hundreds of pastors and lay people. In looking at the Ameri-can laity, he concluded, "But the pastor is not simply reflecting a lack of faith when he voices concern that people are giving less of themselves to his church than they used to. Research has borne out that volunteerism within the church is on the decline."[1]

So there you have it. The pastor is overburdened, the laity is not responding and is under-challenged, and the results distress every-one. In the following chapters we will examine how both pastor and pew-sitter can come to a balanced viewpoint of what needs to be accomplished through the church—and who can do it. We will be looking at how the laity can play a significant role in ministering to their pastor and helping him be the best pastor they've ever had —one who will burn brightly and evenly for the Lord.

Your pastor can have a great sense of fulfillment and support, and an enthusiasm for his ministry. When he does, he will be achiev-ing one of the Lord's main purposes for the church. The goal, wrote the apostle Paul, is for the church—pastor and flock—to "stand firm in one spirit, contending as one man for the faith of the gospel" (Philippians 1:27). This is what pastors are looking for, this is what pastors are praying for; and we sense this is beginning to happen across America as a passion for revival is beginning to penetrate our land.

For pastors to become more effective and less burdened in their God-given ministries, we need to recognize and reject several myths about the pastorate. We have alluded to one, but there are at least eight we church members must recognize. When we expose those myths, then we are better able to help the pastor make the church all God wants it to be. Let's look at those eight myths in chapter 3 and see how we can rid our minds of such faulty thinking about our roles and our pastor's roles in the church.

3

exposing myths
in the pastorate

Sometimes we get a type of image—a stereotype of what someone should be like if he or she is to succeed at a particular job. Then someone comes along and blows the myth to pieces. In sports the image is big, brawny, and fast. And then along comes a Brett Butler. This amazing center fielder, a National League All-Star, led the league in singles four straight years (1992–95). While with the New York Mets, Butler was lauded by manager Dallas Green as having "the right kind of veteran leadership. Brett will lead by example."[1] Butler stands 5 feet 10 inches tall and weighs only 160 pounds, but is one of only two dozen Major League Baseball players to have more than 2,000 hits and 500 stolen bases in his career. He may wear size 7 shoes (the smallest in baseball), but his feet and bat move fast.

Baseball fans may recognize this name. To them, the highlight of Butler's determination and excellence came in 1996, when he went through a battle with throat cancer and yet came back to contribute to another winning record with the Los Angeles Dodgers. Yet Butler endured laughter and disrespect because of his size.

Clearly Butler did not have a fun youth. "Every day for two years," Brett says, "the other kids in junior high would chase me around the playground and try to pull my underwear up above my pants. I would run and run and finally just run home. Every day."

When he played football in high school, they had to go to the junior high school to get his pads because he was so small. He played quarterback and had to roll out just to see over the offensive line. His voice was so high that it cracked when he called the signals, and the opposition would laugh. But his dad told him something he never forgot: "If you don't believe in yourself, nobody else will." That motivated him to give his best.[2]

His high school baseball coach ridiculed him when Brett had the nerve to say he wanted to play baseball at Arizona State, one of the top baseball colleges in the country. But Brett grabbed his glove and went off to Arizona State anyway. He became the leading hitter on their junior varsity team. Yet he was not offered the scholarship he desperately wanted; so he went off to tiny Southeastern Oklahoma State, where he eventually became a two-time All-American. In 1979 he was drafted by the Atlanta Braves organization—in the twenty-third round!

Everyone takes Brett seriously now. He has been recognized as the best bunter in baseball. He steals more than forty bases a year and scores over a hundred runs as well. He's every manager's dream for a lead-off hitter: He hits into double plays only about every two hundred times at bat.

Did Brett Butler make it to the major leagues on the basis of pure athletic ability? Of course not. Here is the secret truth that we need to tell every young person in this land—the very best work harder and overcome the weights they have to carry to make it. It's true in sports, in business, in music, in every endeavor in life. The secret of life is passion, determination, desire.

Enrico Caruso was told by one music teacher, "You can't sing. You have no voice at all." Yet he became one of the best-loved singers of his time.

Beethoven's music teacher said about him, "As a composer he is hopeless."

An editor told Louisa May Alcott that she was incapable of writing anything that would have popular appeal. That, of course, was before *Little Women*.

Walt Disney was once fired by a newspaper editor because he

was thought to have no "good ideas." Tell that to the millions of people thrilled by Walt's movies.

When F. W. Woolworth was twenty-one, he got a job in a store but was not allowed to wait on customers because he "didn't have enough sense."

Each of these famous people proved to have a certain genius— but was it innate or did it grow out of their dedication to developing what they had been given?

WATCH OUT FOR MYTHS

We have seen similarities and have identified common strengths, but every leader, including your pastor, is different. Be careful of buying into myths of what a pastor should have as innate gifts and abilities, of what he should or should not do. Most pastors bear weighty expectations as leaders. Those weights tend to weaken both your pastor's dedication to his calling and his ability to get it done.

The writer of Hebrews recognized this when he wrote of the weights that easily entangle us (12:1). Admittedly he was talking about things that can entangle us that are usually of our own making, but it is just as valid to view those things that come from outside sources as being destructive to the pastor. If they are not lifted, they will keep him from being able to run his race as effectively as God wants him to do.

So what are some of these weights? We believe that much of this weight is due to the myriad of myths that every pastor must learn to overcome. There are dozens of them, but for our purposes here we have selected some of the more devastating. They can launch a pastor into a vicious cycle that leads to despair, discouragement, and even depression. Because pastors love their flock so much, they may easily get their eyes off of what they should be doing and begin to listen to the myriad of voices, especially those echoing the following myths. It is a cycle that becomes a trap.

SEVEN MAJOR MYTHS ABOUT THE PASTOR

Here are seven common myths about the pastor's role in the church.

1. The Pastor Is a Guest of the Church.

The members own the church; the pastor is merely a guest. Despite the fact that the church began as an act of God at Pentecost, many church members sense ownership because of their time and financial investments. For instance, one pastor at an East Coast church had a meeting within the first month of his new pastorate with two of the founders of this local assembly. After pleasant greetings and gracious welcomes, one of the men said something along these lines: "Now, remember, try not to upset the power base. Pastors come and go, but the power base is here forever." Those words can be interpreted to say, "We're glad you're here, but we were here a long time before you, and we will be here a long time after you. If you want your stay to be meaningful and lasting, try not to rock the cart and upset the people who are *really* in control . . . because you aren't."

We can just hear the disciples trying that line on Jesus. "You're going to leave soon, but we're here for the long haul. So please do things our way." Wonder if that is why Peter challenged Jesus' words so often or chose to give Him advice. (See Matthew 16:22; Luke 9:33; John 13:8–9; Acts 11:8.) Or let's put it another way; when was the last time you saw a flock of sheep leading their shepherd? Never? Ridiculous, you say? We agree, but we point out that this myth mindset of the pastor being only a guest leads to just such a problem if it is not corrected.

This incident of the pastor being told he is a guest suggests the possessiveness that many church members feel. If they use the term "our church," they really mean it. Unfortunately, few church members are willing to give their money or invest their time without strings being attached. The church seemingly has forgotten the fact that the Bible says the church belongs to God and we are merely here as agents within the church for its promotion and kingdom impact. Further, through His divine calling, God—not the local congregation—has placed the pastor in charge of the church.

God's Truth and Solution: God set the church up so that power flows from Him to the pastor to the church, not vice versa. We need to respect this order that He has established.

This myth is often referred to as the "country club" mindset. It is the idea that those who have invested the most money and have been members the longest have the most power. The problem is, God never called us to operate a country club. In fact, we should be giving the best to the newest!

2. The Pastor Is Responsible for Asking for Money.

Most pastors believe it is their responsibilty to teach and prepare the congregation for biblical stewardship, yet we know very few pastors who want to be deemed the head fund-raiser. However, many churches think stewardship promotion and pleas for financial giving are solely the responsibility of the pastor. Research continues to show that Christians are giving an ever-decreasing amount of money to their churches. In fact, it has been said that giving today (on a percentage basis) is less than during the Great Depression.

However, if you were to have an informal get-together with a group of pastors, you would not find the number one topic of conversation to be the collection plate. Instead, the number one concern of today's pastors is the overall lack of commitment of the church attendees and their subsequent unwillingness to get involved and to serve. The real problem is not necessarily the priority of giving, nor is it the size of the offering. The problem lies in the members' overall priorities.

God's Truth and Solution: Every church member and attendee must realize that God does not need his or her money. God wants what your money represents—the real you. When your pastor does address the priority of giving, he may be trying gently to remind you of where Christ must be in your life—first place. When Christ is first, then you will have an internal motivation to give because of your love and commitment to Him and His body, the local church. You will count it a privilege and pleasure to see the church prospering and to be a part of all that means.

3. "You Keep Them Humble, Lord; We'll Keep Them Poor."

People may view the salaries and benefits at their personal workplace through one lens and the salaries of the pastoral staff through an entirely different set of lenses. In the minds of too many, pastors and other Christian workers are people who have no right to live comfortably, but should just get by. After all, "They are dedicated to the Lord's work and we don't want them to live an extrava-gant lifestyle." True, extravagance is not what the Lord wants for His servants. But neither does He want them to be barely able to live. It is clear from the Word that "the worker is worth his keep." (Matthew 10:10). Unfortunately, some of the recent money scandals in the Christian community have only served to reinforce the per-ceived need for this negative myth.

Sadly, too many Christians evaluate their ministers by how much it will cost to have them on staff. With this kind of thinking, it doesn't take long for the pastor to become a line item in the budget, and people begin to doubt and question the worth of their shep-herd. "Are we paying him too much? After all, he only works one day a week anyway. Pastors and their families should know, of all people, how to be frugal." We have seen this attitude generate very poor methods of accountability and restrictions. Some pastors are required to provide weekly time sheets for accountability. We have heard of other pastors who were mandated set times for visitation, counseling, and study.

What churches fail to realize is that good pastors save the church money, because poor leadership can and will cost the church.

Because of the abuses of some in Christian leadership, churches have tended to paint all pastors with the same brush. We know a pastor who has qualified for public assistance every year for three years. The reason for such low support? Men in his church say that they are afraid that he will become like some self-indulgent pastor they had read about.

God's Truth and Solution: Only when we are willing to pay a fair salary to our pastors will we get the quality leaders that our churches need. As we bless God's servants, we will experience God's blessing. As pastors who have college-age children, we both know that to be fair to our families, we have to have enough money to give them a good college education. Fortunately for us, our congre-gations feel the same.

4. Change Is a Four-Letter Word.

The future of any entity is often determined by its ability to adapt. The automobile industry moved from big cars to smaller, fuel-efficient cars, from regular to unleaded fuel (thanks to catalytic converters), from metal to plastic auto bodies, all to adapt to the requirements of the public and the government. Businesses in the 1990s call in high-powered consultants to "right-size" the companies and direct its mission. If they are unable to adapt, they will be unable to survive.

The church is under similar pressures. The message of salvation found in "justification by faith" will never change. But unfortunately some churches have become old Edsels, refusing to adapt that unchanging message to the 1990s in order to reach the people who are its inhabitants.

The essence of the Christian life is change—sanctification is the process of changing and becoming more like Jesus, our example. Myth four says that the pastor should not be an agent of change. Yet prayer and preaching mandate a willingness to change. A pastor's entire ministry involves maturing individuals and the church family, which requires change.

Like our pastors today, Jesus faced the same problem—resistance to change—when He ministered. The Pharisees did not accept Him. "He heals on the Sabbath! Horrors! We cannot change that feature of our religious thought. It has never been allowed and we will not allow it ever." Now, had God said, "Thou shalt not heal on a Sabbath," then they would have been dead right. But they were instead dead in their traditions—traditions that came from men, Jesus pointed out.

Don't get us wrong; we believe tradition is important, but only when it does not impede God's work. Jesus recognized this when He ministered in a different way in order to reach people like the Samaritan woman. He knew that the tradition of not talking to a woman when you are a rabbi (teacher), and definitely not as a Jew associating with Samaritans, was not from God, but rather was a tradition of man. That is why He violated man's traditions in order to carry out God's work in the middle of change.

Unfortunately, today we have forgotten that the essence of the Christian life is change, as we become more like Christ (2 Corinthians 4:16). To pray is to open myself up to change, to worship is to open my life up to change, to be progressively changed . . . more and more into the image of Christ. To mature is to change; the same thing is true of the local church. To not change is to die. We need to recognize that there is only one thing that is constant—change—and if not faced, the work of God and the church will struggle and fail to accomplish all God wants done.

In working with one church, we remember the elder board asking for assistance in determining why so many young couples were leaving their church. These elders were challenged to do "exit polls" on these couples, interviewing them to make a proper diagnosis. The elders were sent out in twos and polled seven couples. Without exception, all seven couples loved the church, the pastor, and the programs. Then why did they leave? One couple said, "We'd probably come back if you spruced up the baby care." The median age of this elder board was mid-sixties, so they had not been in the nursery for many years. No new leaders had been incorporated into the leadership for fear of change, and they were not aware of the peeling wallpaper, broken toys, and need for new furniture. This elder board discovered what many are learning: change is *not* a four-letter word.

God's Truth and Solution: Change can be a blessing in disguise, which can lead to spiritual health, strengthening of the ministry, and accomplishing all God wants from the local church. Seek God on change. Let Him show you how to adapt to changing situations.

5. Preaching Is Only to Be Heard.

High on the list of expectations for the typical pastoral search committee is preaching. We have never spoken in a church that did not want a good preacher. But few churches realize what makes for a good sermon and good preaching Sunday after Sunday. Most people come to church after a busy and highly pressured week simply to listen; often they are passive. They do not desire to do anything with what they have heard.

In part, this comes from a misconception of why we listen to the pastor in the first place. To people who choose to be passive, the motivation for attending may simply be one of habit: "I've always attended church." They come with little expectations, and their expectations are not disappointed.

Most pastors are trained at seminaries to apply the Word of God to the listeners through their preaching. Indeed, the pastor's role in preaching and teaching is to see that every believer is challenged to be "thoroughly equipped for every good work" (2 Timothy 3:17). In order for this to happen the pastor must point out the relevancy of the Word of God to contemporary life and call his people to an active response. This requires the congregation to be open, ready to evaluate areas of life that may need change in order to be conformed to God's Word.

God's Truth and Solution: God can speak to you through each sermon. He then expects you to apply His truths to your daily living. What church attendees also need to recognize is that the manner in which they listen to a sermon greatly influences the pastor's delivery and the message's personal impact. We have spoken in African-American churches where members make every sermon great because they are willing to participate while listening. A wise old pastor once shared, "Preaching should never be a spectator sport."

6. Pastors Are the Sole Encouragers.

There must be some unwritten law: "The pastor must always be up and must encourage everyone else." However, like everything else in life, ministry can be painful and discouraging. Pastors are criticized, their families are criticized, and their ministries are criticized. Yes, we know, this goes with the territory, but pastors also need encouragement. Why do you think so many pastors take Mondays off? To hide!! We know pastors who regularly receive hate-mail, both signed and unsigned. We know pastors who regularly have Sunday's bulletin on their desk with corrections circled in red and others who are grasped in the hallway right before they preach to be nailed with a complaint. We know far too many pastors who have burned out trying to please everyone but pleasing no one. Remember, there is no such thing as a narrow-minded, nit-picking encourager.

God's Truth and Solution: The Bible is filled with one-anothers. We need to love one another, bear one another's burdens, forgive one another, be kind one to another, among others. Pastors are a part of a larger body . . . your church. Will they make mistakes? Absolutely, but encourage them. Will they make bad decisions?

Without a doubt, but encourage them. A pat on the back will never hinder their performance. You could make your pastor's day just by choosing to be an encourager to the one God has called to lead you.

7. All Mistakes Are the Pastor's Fault.

"Anything that goes wrong is the pastor's fault." This myth is so widespread that it is like Cinderella's glass slipper—people are shocked to learn the shoe doesn't fit. Most people feel the pastor has the final say in everything, so he has the blame for what goes wrong, too. But is that fair? Is this what we do in our families? Do we blame the parents for *all* the misbehavior of their children, or do we give them some leeway, knowing that free will fits in there somewhere?

God's Truth and Solution: Yes, the pastor has much responsibility, but he is not responsible for every action of every church member done in the name of the church. He can help to set safeguards through reporting and clear guidelines for service, but the bottom line is that the church is made up of individuals who are part of a body and often function with some degree of autonomy. We need to give the pastor some grace when it comes to finding who is at fault for negative happenings.

GOOD INTENTIONS

When Glen first started coaching the girls' softball team at Redondo High School, he always met the team bus in the school parking lot. The team and assistant coach boarded the bus, and the off-campus coach traveled to away games in his own car so he could return home more quickly afterward. Of course, Glen had no idea where the other schools were located, so he'd follow the team bus closely. He would draft behind the bus and make the same turns to find the host school. The only problem with this approach was that Glen often would get separated. And do you know how many yellow buses there are on the road at 2 P.M. in southern California?

One day the Redondo Seahawks had an away game at Beverly Hills High School, and once again Glen got separated from the bus; but later he caught up to what he thought was the right bus. He didn't bother to notice who was on the bus or the number of the bus; he simply followed.

The bus arrived at an elementary school in Westminster; only then did Glen realize what he had done. He finally found the Beverly Hills campus and barely made it in time for the game, which he was coaching.

In reading this chapter on the myths of the pastorate, one could easily say, "So what? What does it matter as long as you are sincere?" The truth is that you can be sincere, but you can be sincerely wrong. Glen had good intentions, but he still went the wrong way. He still got lost. The fact is, it takes more than sincerity to make it in life or to have a successful ministry. It takes truth. And knowing the truth includes exposing the myths of the pastorate. When it comes to the pastor and his flock, we must recognize the importance of teamwork and biblical unity. We will begin to understand this premise in chapter 4, as we identify the pastor's role in the process.

4

the pastor's role

After the 1992 Los Angeles riots, reporter Steve Futterman of CBS radio interviewed one of the riot's looters. The man had been one of many people who had looted a record store. When asked what he had stolen, the man replied, "Gospel tapes. I love Jesus."[1]

Too often that is the picture the world sees of what a Christian is all about. Yet Jesus defined His followers as the "salt of the earth." Jesus never told them that one day they would become the salt of the earth, but rather they were already the "salt of the earth." Salt was a valuable commodity in the culture of these disciples to whom Jesus was speaking. Salt was the primary means for preserving food before refrigeration. Salt was also an antiseptic vital to the cleaning of wounds and fighting infection. Today salt continues to play a vital role, as it brings out what is inherent within the food. It causes flavors to be heightened.

Thus, what Jesus is telling these disciples and us today is that once people become followers of Jesus, there is no turning back. He has designed us to enhance what is good around us, to help in the healing of wounds, to preserve what is good, and to fight that which tries to destroy those around us.

WHY THE CHURCH EXISTS

The church, the body of Christ, exists to glorify the Savior. Significantly, the modern pastor has a crucial role in preparing church members, followers of Jesus, to honor Christ. He equips them for service, one of three vital purposes of the church. Let's briefly explore all three.

1. Redemption

God has placed the church on earth for several reasons. First, it is a place of redemption. The true church is a place where the unbeliever can hear how to enter into a right relationship with God. Too frequently the church has lost this message and has become only a place for fellowship and where you can find new clients for your insurance business. Fellowship is important; in fact, it is also a function of the true church (see below); but salvation must come first. Without a redeemed life, the church becomes nothing more than a social club; so-called "fellowship" becomes only inconsequential social chatter. Too many churches today have "lost their savor" by allowing themselves to be contaminated by the world's ways and have lost their God-given direction and purpose.

God designed the church to be light to those living in darkness, to be salt to those who are perishing. The church has to keep its priorities in place if it is to be all that God intends it to be.

2. Fellowship

Second, it is a place for fellowship. Yes, spiritual fellowship is important. The church can provide a wonderful setting for believers to meet together, to enjoy the company of people of like mind, and to learn spiritually from each other. We are to meet together (see Hebrews 10:25) for several reasons:

- We are more vulnerable to enemy attacks if we are in a battle alone.
- Being together helps us keep a healthy perspective.
- We can be salt and light to each other as we encourage one another from our own experiences and pray for the needs of other believers.

- It is harder for Satan to pick people off when they are in a healthy, supporting group. It is the loner who becomes easy prey for enemy attacks.

3. Equipping

Third, the church is a place to equip the Christian to live as a Christian, share as a Christian, and serve as a Christian. Paul wrote to the church in Ephesus that Jesus "gave some to be apostles, some to be prophets, some to be evangelists, and some to be pastors and teachers, to prepare God's people for works of service, so that the body of Christ may be built up until we all reach unity in the faith and in the knowledge of the Son of God and become mature, attaining to the whole measure of the fullness of Christ" (Ephesians 4:11–13).

Why does the church need a pastor? Because pastors have a biblical mandate to prepare, to equip God's people to serve with Him as they are equipped. This equipping can be a twofold process: first repairing, then preparing for something greater in ministry. The word for "prepare" in Ephesians 4 is the Greek word *katartidzo*. By examining the many uses of this word in the New Testament, we can gain a clearer understanding of the call of the pastor and his role and why God uses a pastor to challenge the people to accomplish all that God wants them to do. Frank Tillapaugh once wrote, "Pastor-teachers are to train lay men and women to minister to the world. They in turn are to train others and the work continues."[2]

WHY THE PASTOR MUST EQUIP THE PEOPLE

The church may believe this principle, but it rarely tries to practice it. The church may be convinced of the "priesthood of the believer," but its members tend to practice the "priesthood of the priesthood." Ephesians 4:11–12 indicates that God appoints ministers to equip the saints for ministry. Ultimately Christ is the head of the church, but He has placed "undershepherds" with the primary function of bringing people under the authority of Christ, the Scriptures, and the church, in order that the people might serve others as well.

The Need for Leadership

One of the truths about humans is we need structure; we need leadership. An effective university is led by a school president, not by the students. An effective chief executive officer, one who can sort through the reports and with input from all departments and other leaders make the final decision, usually makes the right decisions. He's been trained to do so, despite the issues and tensions that may swirl around him.

Human nature shows that man left to himself to decide what to do without leadership will gravitate to mediocrity. Societal pressures have caused such changes, and few want to take a stand or draw a line in the sand to say "this far and no farther." God knows our weaknesses. This is why He established the pastor as leader. There has to be someone responsible, who is qualified to lead and who is willing to do so.

Like a Shepherd

God has been careful in the Bible to define the role of the pastor in a way that is rich with meaning. He is called the *shepherd* (Acts 20:28; 1 Peter 5:2). For a moment, let's consider the metaphor of the shepherd, which our clergy, or pastors, are to emulate. The shepherd has a primary task of caring for the sheep. If the shepherd is to fulfill his task, he must provide the boundaries in which there is safety and all the resources necessary for life. He will lead them in safe paths; the sheep will only face danger if they remove themselves from his care and his wise boundaries.

Remember, a shepherd leads the flock where it needs to go. He may walk beside it or behind it or in front of it, but he is always leading it. At times the flock moves in the right direction for a long time without any direct control or correction by the shepherd. But, after a while, the shepherd will need to exercise some control and authority in turning it or stopping it or urging it on faster. The shepherd leads gently and patiently, choosing the best paths and pastures, constantly watching the sheep that would wander off from the flock.

Similarly, a pastor leads the church gently, patiently, yet firmly. He watches where the church is headed to be sure that it is going in the right direction. The pastor's tasks may not always be exciting. In fact, at times, he may lead by a quiet, settled approach; but his is a very important work for the church. The church needs its pastors to lead.

Two well-known seminary professors—we'll call them Jim and Phil—once traveled together around the world. As they were going to their plane, they came to the swinging doors.

"After you, Jim."

"No, after you, Phil."

Bystanders heard the two repeat those words for almost a minute. Those two men were stuck at the door, neither one wanting to surrender his will to the other and be in the position of letting the other go last.

"By the time we got to the plane, we realized that one of us had to be designated the leader," Jim explained later. "So we took turns."

A cute (and true) story, but one that has a definite point: God designed man to have one person be the leader, even when they are peers. This is true even in the Godhead, it is true in the family, and it is true in the church. Things work best when one person has "the buck stop here."

SIX PRIMARY WAYS
PASTORS EQUIP THE CHURCH

The Scriptures teach that the pastor is God's chosen instrument to lead the church. God knew that we needed one person to be responsible before Him, through whom He could guide and direct His church at each local level. This has been true in history from at least the times of Moses and the prophets; it continues today. This is why He established the role of pastor.

There are six main ways that God uses the pastor to equip the church. *Equip* means to prepare, and as the leader, the pastor prepares his flock to minister. As we noted earlier, the pastor equips the flock to do the work of ministry. Here are six ways he does that.

1. The Pastor As a Healing Agent

In Ephesians 4:12, we find the only use of the word *katartismos,* meaning "preparing or equipping;" yet there is a rich history behind this word in classical Greek writings.[3] One use is the description of a doctor resetting a bone. This may have either meant the reduction of a fracture[4] or the realignment of a bone out of socket. Thus one pastoral ministry is to see that members of the church, Christ's body, are rightly connected to one another. The pastor should help to restore broken relationships.

A vivid example of this pastoral call occurs in the book of Acts. Saul, once an enemy of the church and certainly someone to be avoided, had become a Christian. A new, positive relationship was needed between the leaders in Jerusalem and this new convert, whom they distrusted. The leadership was afraid to enfold Saul (who later became Paul), when along came Barnabas.

"Barnabas took him and brought him to the apostles. He told them how Saul on his journey had seen the Lord and that the Lord had spoken to him, and how in Damascus he had preached fearlessly in the name of Jesus" (Acts 9:27). The once dislocated limb of the body was now rightly in place where effective ministry and service could take place.

A modern-day version of the healing of a broken body comes when the pastor is involved in counseling. For instance, the minister will help a husband and wife who are about to fracture their marriage to find the biblical principles that can bring forgiveness and healing. Many a happily married couple today can trace back their currently healthy relationship to a time when the pastor was used of God to repair their torn relationship and help bring about permanent healing. This same scenario is often played out as the pastor helps parents restore their relationship with rebellious children who are tearing at the fabric of the family unity. We love to listen to fellow pastors who have godly discernment as they help those who are hurting find biblical healing for their wounds.

2. The Pastor As a Repairing Agent

The two fishermen, James and John, awoke early, had a quick bite to eat, and headed toward the Sea of Galilee to maintain their livelihood. Matthew 4:21 (NASB) records, "Going on from there He saw two other brothers, James the son of Zebedee, and John his brother, in the boat with Zebedee their father, mending their nets;

and He called them." Notice they were "mending" (*katartizontas*) their nets. These nets needed repairing if they were ever to be of any service again. If left unprepared, not cleaned of the seaweed, sticks, and debris, the water would fail to pass through; thus the fish would never swim in their direction. If the nets were left broken and torn, the fish would pass right through. The nets needed to be repaired. Likewise the believers in the church often find themselves in need of repair to be able to serve adequately. This repair may include more than just initial training. This may also involve a redirection of attitudes toward the tasks God may wish them to perform.

Consider Paul, who had written a glaring charge to this church in his previous letter (1 Corinthians 5:1–5) and was desperately anticipating some kind of response. He then traveled to Greece to look for one of his younger colleagues, Titus. In 2 Corinthians 7:6 we read, "But God, who comforts the downcast, comforted us by the coming of Titus." Titus was able to repair Paul's spirit and help him find enough strength to continue in his ministry. Here were two fellow pilgrims, followers of Christ, mending the nets for the subsequent fishing up ahead.

Today many a pastor is used of the Lord to counsel and disciple, to direct both staff and church leadership so that they can make any necessary "midcourse corrections" in their ministries, and thus accomplish what God has gifted them to do and be. And one need not be in leadership, either. Most of us know those who can point to a time in their lives when their pastor said just the right thing that kept them from a disaster. The pastor who listens to God is a sharp instrument in His hands to convey His truth and His healing in lives.

3. The Pastor As a Building Agent

In the Septuagint, the Greek translation of the Old Testament, our word *katartizo* is used on several occasions to represent the rebuilding of the wall of Jerusalem and the Temple.[5] Judah found itself in captivity and the Temple had been totally decimated. But Israel was allowed to return and rebuild. Israel's opponents wrote the king: "The king should know that the Jews who came up to us from you have gone to Jerusalem and are rebuilding that rebellious and wicked city. They are restoring the walls and repairing the foundations" (Ezra 4:12). The word picture is one of taking the broken-down stones and placing them back in an orderly manner.

In the life of any church there will be periods when it's necessary to rebuild and help believers to get back into their "correct order." For instance, in Galatians 6:1 we are told that we are to rebuild the lives of those who are caught in sin and cannot find release or relief. Thus we are to restore them in a spirit of gentleness. But beyond restoring and repairing, there will be the making of new "bricks" for the building, of expanding the current walls to encompass even more area the Lord has for your church. The pastor, as the building agent, helps to select potentially valuable, new building materials. As new believers become a part of the body, the pastor is there in part to oversee their accurate placement in the body so that a rectangular brick does not get placed in a square space.

4. The Pastor As a Change Agent

The pastor also is an agent for change in his people; this can be seen in a variety of passages dealing with the concept of *completion* of believers.[6] The word carries the "notion of making complete, which can include making complete by restoring or training."[7]

The Bible was given to us to generate change in our lives, not just to create intellectual assent. The pastor equips his people by helping and guiding them toward change, so they may become and remain effective servants of God and instruments of change in their spheres of influence.

A great illustration of this principle can be found in Acts. Apollos was an intelligent and very teachable man, yet he understood little about the ways of Christ; he only knew of the baptism of John (Acts 18:25). Seeing the need for a change of thinking in Apollos' life, Aquilla and Priscilla approached Apollos; they were willing to explain the ways of God accurately and clearly. The result was that Apollos was sent off on a mission, changed and prepared.

The pastor becomes an agent of change as he challenges people to greater heights and deeper walks in their Christian life. He often will be able to see the gifting of an individual or sense a need to challenge a person to a greater level of commitment. Because of the position God has given the pastor in the church, his words of challenge often receive more weight and are heeded more quickly than those of a Christian friend or acquaintance.

5. The Pastor As a Prayer Agent

In-depth prayer does not always come easily for the pastor, yet it is one of the most important parts of his personal as well as ministry life. When you and other worshipers observe your leader modeling prayer's importance in every area, you will, as good sheep, follow his lead and give prayer a higher priority in your own lives.

After all, isn't this just what Jesus did? His life was saturated with prayer—early mornings, during ministry, evenings—at times all night. (See, for example, Mark 1:35; 6:46; 14:32–40.)

Here's a key question: If you could have Jesus personally teach you *anything,* what would you ask Him for? How to perform miracles? How to cast out demons or deal well with Satan? Perhaps it would be "How can I be a great evangelist?" (or perhaps a great teacher). It might be "How can I disciple people in a dynamic, effective way?" Or "How can I earn great quantities of money to put into ministry?" These are all things that come to mind, we'll admit. But what did Jesus' own "sheep"—His disciples—ask Him to teach them? The only thing they ever asked to be taught was how to pray (Luke 11:1). They recognized the pivotal role prayer played in Jesus' life. We are convinced that this is why they asked to learn how to pray.

So we can see the strategic positioning God has given to the pastor. He is the undershepherd, responsible for the nurturing and care of those God brings into His church. When the congregation responds to a prayerful pastor, then there is a natural flow of God's wisdom. When our pastors perform in the capacity and role God has given them, His help is channeled through them to us, His people.

6. The Pastor As a Cohesive Agent

Your pastor often is the main "glue" the Lord uses to hold the church together. When he is a "strong glue," he is able to promote vision and unity, to be the one everyone wants to follow. He in essence says, "Follow me," just as Paul told people to follow his example, and as Jesus, our Shepherd, said to follow Him. A good pastor will provide a stabilizing factor for the church.

That is why churches too often struggle when they lose a good pastor. If the position is left vacant too long, there can be significant problems to continued growth and stability. It is a rare church that is able to survive untouched if it remains too long without a pastor. Just as a child can survive without a parent, so a church can survive without a pastor, but not at the same level of competence. This is how God has designed His church. The pastor "parents" the local body and becomes to it much of what Jesus is to the universal body. The pastor sets the course, the tone, the very fabric design of the church.

Think of the influence of a pastor. A good one can leave a healthy, thriving church as he moves on to a new congregation. But when his replacement comes, if he is not up to the standard the church needs, the church may and usually does go downhill very quickly.

In fact, you can say that the church is similar to a lighthouse in its community. The pastor is the light—the first strong thing people see when they come—and his guidance becomes a beacon to newcomers and often a deciding factor on whether they stay or leave.

BEING A USABLE PERSON FOR GOD

If you did not desire to make an impact with your life for God and His kingdom, you would not be reading this book. So we can assume God has placed upon your heart the burden to make a difference in your church. Some of you, however, have approached this section a little intimidated because you do not feel adequately trained or appropriately talented to tackle the assignment God might give you.

Jesus told a wonderful parable concerning the usability of people for the kingdom of God in Matthew 25. Jesus was a master at using illustrations of simple things to make eternal points. In Matthew 25:14–29, the parable of the talents, He illustrated how important it is to use the gifts God has given us. Jesus told of "a man going on a journey, who called his servants and entrusted his property to them." He gave three servants varying amounts of money—

one five talents, another two, and the final just one talent. The amounts were given based on the ability of each one (verse 15).

After "a long time," the master returned and asked for an account of how each handled his portion. The man who had been entrusted with five talents had been able to return ten. The one given two returned four. The master expressed his strong approval for the first two, telling them they were "good and faithful" servants. He then rewarded them according to their labor and invited them to share in their master's happiness.

But the one given one talent returned the very one he had been given, unused and with no multiplication. He told his master, "I knew that you are a hard man, harvesting where you have not sown and gathering where you have not scattered seed. So I was afraid and went out and hid your talent in the ground. See, here is what belongs to you." Jesus, through the words of the master, expressed His view of those who hide or bury their God-given talents. "You wicked, lazy servant! So you knew that I harvest where I have not sown and gather where I have not scattered seed? Well then, you should have put my money on deposit with the bankers, so that when I returned I would have received it back with interest."

The master then instructed a servant to "take the talent from him and give it to the one who has the ten talents." Jesus summed up the point by having the master say these sobering words: "For everyone who has will be given more, and he will have an abundance. Whoever does not have, even what he has will be taken from him."

What principles can be drawn from this parable which can enable everyone in the church to become a more usable person? The message is clear: Use it or lose it! But note also that, as in the example of Moses and the battle, use it in whatever way God gives you an opportunity, or we all lose!

We depend on each other. Our Moses—our pastors—cannot lead alone. They need others to come alongside to assist and encourage. We do not need to be highly qualified. We need only be willing to lift his arms. We need only help him help others.

Each church needs a pastor—one who wants to lead, one whom His sheep want to follow. Such a pastor can be used of the Lord to equip *your* church to be all God wants it to be, to shepherd his congregation in a way that will help establish Christ's kingdom in a stronger way through the local body of believers.

Let us now turn our focus on one of those opportunities to encourage your pastor's heart. It represents two of the most important ways any church member can help his pastor: he can pray for the pastor, and he can help to silence those who might be murmuring or trying to attack the leader without reason.

5

preyed on
or prayed for

This chapter title is not original with us. *Preyed on or Prayed for*, a book we love, brings into focus the picture in many churches: The pastor is either being upheld in prayer by his sheep, or else his sheep are trying to bite him. As the book's author, Terry Teykle, explains:

> Sheep can bite. In fact, they can knock you [the pastor] down, stomp on you and drag you into the bushes for dead. If you have ever pastored, you know this to be true. Just move their table, bring a guitar into the sanctuary or change the order of the service, and they come at you with teeth bared and fire in their eyes! Go to any denominational preachers' meeting and listen to the pastors, and they will show the scars and teeth marks left by irate sheep. Sheep *can* bite.[1]

Now sheep are not the smartest animals in the world. Sometimes sheep have even followed the lead sheep over a cliff, hesitating only slightly. The same thing can happen with human sheep. Sometimes, as we saw in chapter 3, the pastor can have sheep who push great weights upon him in addition to those weights that naturally come with the job of pastor. Sometimes sheep get a wrong idea in their mind—like unjust criticism—and they follow that critical path until they fall over the edge of a cliff, tragically taking along with them other sheep and at times even the shepherd. In the church we call this a "church split."

HELPFUL SHEEP

Gossip, criticism, and the like are all too common in our churches today. So how do we help stop these negative things from occurring? Obviously, the first thing is not to engage in it or let others pull you into their negative thinking. Satan, our enemy, is the accuser of the brethren (Revelation 12:10). He will do everything he can to plant negative thoughts in the minds of unaware sheep. He will use their pride to act as a decoy to get them to follow his thinking and therefore pull the unsuspecting flock of sheep over the cliff.

But we can be the sheep God uses to help stop such a catastrophe. We can use the powerful element of prayer to intercept and even expose the accuser of the brethren, who is roaming around, looking for those whom he can devour (1 Peter 5:8). Prayer has long been recognized as one of the most essential instruments God has given us to stop enemy attacks. The wonderful thing is that we can use it not only for ourselves but also for others. We call this type of praying "intercession; we are asking God on the behalf of others for things we know He wants done in their lives.

When it comes to our pastors and those in leadership, we often use the terms "hedging in," "prayer shield," "putting a wall of protection," or other similar phrases to indicate that prayer is helping stop what otherwise might attack our leaders.

PRAYING FOR GODLY LEADERS

Is this an idea we have recently developed? Is it something only for the weaker leaders? No, we see Paul asking for prayer for himself. This independent, highly qualified, very knowledgeable disciple felt the absolute necessity of having prayers offered on his behalf. Was this simply a psychological thing, wherein he felt better if he knew people were praying and/or hoped that a lot of prayer might persuade God to do something? Was it some clever way to get people on his side by having them go through a routine of praying for him, even though he knew their prayers had no real influence on God?

Indeed not! Paul knew the power of prayer. He recognized the valuable partnership that comes through prayer. To the Roman believers he wrote: "I urge you, brothers, by our Lord Jesus Christ and by the love of the Spirit, to join me in my struggle by praying to God for me" (Romans 15:30). He then mentioned some of the areas for which he needed specific prayers. Similarly, He wrote the Thessalonian believers: "Brothers, pray for us" (1 Thessalonians 5:25). But he recognized it was a partnership; he prayed for them as well. "We always thank God for all of you, mentioning you in our prayers," he told the Thessalonians (1 Thessalonians 1:2). To other churches he said the same type of things concerning prayer. (See Philippians 1:9; Colossians 1:9.)

Even the prayers of individuals had an impact on Paul's life and what God could do. This is seen in Philemon 22, where he wrote, "I hope to be restored to you in answer to your prayers." Paul gave credit where credit was due. He well could have said, "I love you so much that I am taking time out of my hectic schedule to come see you." Instead he says he is coming, but it is because Philemon has prayed. He acknowledged a partnership that was influencing how God chose to order Paul's steps and where he would minister. We see the same ideas expressed in 2 Corinthians 1:10–11, where Paul anticipated God's deliverance "as you help us by your prayers."

So we are on good, solid, biblical grounds when we choose to pray for our pastors. And believe us, they *really* need those prayers.

THE PRAYER LIFE OF A PASTOR

Take a quick quiz. Try to guess how many minutes a day the average pastor of the nineties prays. Did you guess three and one-half minutes?[2] If you didn't, you lose. Actually, we all lose when our pastors do not pray the way that God has intended. Is this sparse time in prayer because pastors don't want to pray or don't know how to pray? We don't think so. In the conversations we've had with pastors, the suffering prayer lives often are due to their lives and ministries being driven by a myriad of tasks. Although focusing on a different aspect of ministry, Woodrow Kroll, general director of Back to the Bible, believes a pastor's meager prayer life is connected to ministry involvement. "I fear that growing numbers of pastors today are so weighed down with the details and problems of the ministry that they have lost meaningful contact with the people around them."[3]

We've come to the key of any pastor's success, the heart of his strength, the most important thing in the life of any pastor, and yet too frequently the most vulnerable—his prayer life. Every other area can be strong, but if this one is weak, he is weak no matter how strong he may seem in any other respect.

We often think that pastors are spiritual giants, able to pray down God's power for any problem that arises. When we think of those we want to pray for us in a time of crisis, it is natural to think of asking our pastors, especially when we know them on a first-name basis. But even if you don't, you still may go forward at the end of a service and ask his prayers for your burdens.

However, as experienced pastors, we can tell you that few pastors, ourselves included, feel qualified to pray "powerfully" for the many requests that come. We can barely cover our own needs, let alone those of our church family. Yes, we know prayer is vital. No, we do not feel capable or skilled enough in prayer to be able to pray the kinds of prayers that will release God's corrective power into each crisis we know about. Our hearts break over sin and its consequences—broken homes, hurt children, sickness, damaged relationships, misunderstandings, blocked dreams, etc. The list is unending of things we see that need strong prayer undergirding.

BATTLES IN PRAYER

We find, as do all our sheep, that it is a real battle to be able to pray properly. This battle, this spiritual warfare, is one of the most intense any pastor faces. Yet few recognize it as warfare. In fact, we are convinced that the spiritual warfare that surrounds prayer is more intense than that directed against evangelism. Those who know the power of prayer recognize that it is at the heart of everything God does here on earth. People don't get saved unless others pray for them. Church growth is inhibited without prayer; problems don't get permanently solved in our lives unless, through prayer, we bring God into the situation.

Satan is no fool. He knows that if he can stop prayer, he will short-circuit God's power in the person's life and weaken the impact God would have brought upon the focus of those prayers. Sadly, for far too many of us, pastors included, the enemy has been effective in neutralizing our prayer lives.

PRIORITIES FOR THE PASTOR'S PRAYER LIFE

So, what does God expect of the pastor in his prayer life? We believe God has three priorities for the pastor's prayer life: his relationship with God, his ongoing prayers, and being a prayer discipler. You can pray for each of these areas on behalf of your pastor.

The Highest Priority: Relationship with God

The highest priority God has for the pastor is that *he put talking to God and establishing a close relationship with Him above every other priority—above ministry, above family, above his own desires.* The Lord tells every follower to seek Him with all of one's heart (Deuteronomy 4:29). As part of this, worship should be a key element.

In other words, your pastor needs to spend *quality* time with the Lord, not just a brief "Hello, glad You're with me today in all I do" expression. The Lord wants your pastor to be like David, whose shepherd's heart longed for much time with the Chief Shepherd. "One thing I ask of the Lord, this is what I seek: that I may dwell in the house of the Lord all the days of my life, to gaze upon the beauty of the Lord and to seek him in his temple . . . My heart says of you, 'Seek his face!' Your face, Lord, I will seek" (Psalm 27:4, 8).

David was one smart guy. He sought the Lord for who God is, worshiping, praising, and loving Him. But David also knew that in doing so, other benefits would come. After declaring his desire to dwell in God's house in worship, David added, "For in the day of trouble he will keep me safe in his dwelling; he will hide me in the shelter of his tabernacle and set me high upon a rock. Then my head will be exalted above the enemies who surround me; at his tabernacle will I sacrifice with shouts of joy" (27:5–6).

The Need to Pray Always

Another element God expects to be part of the pastor's prayer life is that *he pray about everything in his life and does it continually.*

+ *And pray in the Spirit on all occasions with all kinds of prayers and requests. With this in mind, be alert and always keep on praying for all the saints.* (Ephesians 6:18)

+ *Pray continually.* (1 Thessalonians 5:17)

Such ongoing prayers are God's standard for *all* His children. But for the pastor it is an absolute must. It is through prayer and as he studies the Word and prays about what he is reading that he will know the heart of God and be able to understand God's leading for himself and for his people. Through prayer he will be strengthened in order to withstand the many assaults of the enemy, hold up under the numerous burdens, and cope with the sudden disasters that touch the lives of his people and possibly his own family. Only through prayer will he be able to maintain his cool in the midst of the hot arguments and strong, even bitter, disagreements that too often are part of pastoring a church.

Your pastor is like Peter walking on the water. As long as he keeps his eyes on the Lord through prayer, he will be able to walk on top of the deepest waters. But the second he gets his eyes off the Lord and focuses on the problems and/or negative people, he will start sinking. So he needs to saturate everything with meaningful, God-led prayer.

Being a Prayer Discipler

God also expects the pastor to become a discipler in prayer. This means *he needs to model how to pray* as well as teach it. Both the Old and New Testaments declare God's strong desire for prayer to be the heart of the church, the thing for which it is known. In fact it is Jesus Himself who makes it crystal clear when He reminds His listeners of God's intention: "My house will be called a house of prayer" (Matthew 21:13, quoting Jeremiah 7:11). The pastor is the one who carries on the work of Jesus with the congregation as its undershepherd or leader. Leaders have followers. To be a follower means to walk in the steps of the one leading, or at least alongside the leader.

Therefore, for the congregation and the church as a whole to have a strong, healthy prayer life, the pastor must take the initiative in modeling prayer. He should desire and see that prayer is at the heart of everything the church does. Only when this occurs will the church truly be a house of prayer and fulfill God's strong desire for His body.

The Scriptures are full of examples of the chosen leader modeling prayer for the people. David readily comes to mind with so many of the Psalms being his written prayers. Nehemiah modeled the strong need for prayer both on a private and open basis before the people (Nehemiah 1:4,11). Ezra prayed publicly with passion and repentance after hearing of the sins of the people (Ezra 9). Paul is a consummate example of a leader modeling prayer. He wrote frequently of his prayers for people and his requests for their prayers. "We constantly pray for you, that our God may count you worthy of his calling, and that by his power he may fulfill every good purpose of yours and every act prompted by your faith" (2 Thessalonians 1:11. See also Philippians 1:9; Colossians 1:9; 1 Thessalonians 5:23–25; 2 Thessalonians 3:1–3; Hebrews 13:18.)

Unfortunately, in our fast-paced, twenty-first century mind-set, the less visible, time-consuming area of prayer often suffers in the life of the average pastor. Remember the three and one-half minutes? How can we help them?

HOW TO HELP YOUR PASTOR

Have a Right Perspective

We need to have a right perspective of who our pastors are. They are ordinary people who have responded to the call of God to be our leaders, our undershepherds. They are not perfect; they encounter the same temptations as you and I do. Only the indwelling of the Holy Spirit gives them the ability to succeed. And the only thing that truly sets them apart from others is the distinct call of the Lord on their lives and their resulting amount of yielding to the Lord's control. Yet they must live to a higher standard than others. The Bible clearly says, "From everyone who has been given much, much will be required" (Luke 12:48 NASB). Since prayer does not come easily, and is a battleground for pastors, we can have a significant part in helping them.

As we've already seen, Paul requested prayers. And recall that Moses, one of the most dynamic Old Testament leaders, needed the support of his disciples as he "interceded" to God. Aaron and Hur had to prop his hands up as he held them up to God during the battle Joshua and his men were fighting (Exodus 17).

You can be an Aaron or Hur for your pastor in the work God has asked of him. You can hold his hands up, for without help, he will never be able to do what God has asked him to do. That is one of the beautiful things about being in a family, being part of the body of Christ. Each member is related to another; each can help the other to better perform his or her part in the body.

So let's look at your role in praying for your pastor.

Two Kinds of Prayers

You can pray for your pastor in two ways. First, pray for the priority of prayer in his life and ministry. Second, pray for specific needs in various areas of his life and ministry. In praying for him, it is helpful to use appropriate Scripture as the foundation upon which you are praying and to reinforce the rightness of your requests.

Here are a few key verses to recall as you pray for your pastor:

+ *Therefore encourage one another and build up one another, just as you also are doing. But we request of you, brethren, that you appreciate those who diligently labor among you, and have charge over you in the Lord and give you instruction, and that you esteem them very highly in love because of their work. Live in peace with one another.* (1 Thessalonians 5:11–13 NASB)

+ *Pray also for me, that whenever I open my mouth, words may be given me so that I will fearlessly make known the mystery of the gospel.* (Ephesians 6:19)

Too often we pray simple, generalized prayers that have little impact on our pastor and fall far below the level of prayer that a pastor needs. You know, "Lord, bless the pastor this day. Help him in everything he does. Protect him and give him wisdom in all he does." Nice, but not powerful. Your pastor is in the midst of a spiritual battle. As David Fisher says, "Fiery darts come from all directions seen and unseen, making pastoral ministry a wearying task."[4] So how should we pray?

In 1 John 5 we are told to pray according to God's will, and that if we do so, we can then know that He will answer. How can you guarantee you are praying according to God's will for your pastor? By praying scripturally based prayers, adapting them for your pastor. (For example, consider praying through Ephesians 3:14–21, replacing "you" with your pastor's name.)

PRAYERS FOR YOUR PASTOR'S LIFE AND MINISTRY

We have identified several areas that are important to target with prayer, especially scripturally based prayers. In this section we provide sample prayers (in italicized script) based on specific verses to deal with key areas in your pastor's ministry.

You will notice that sometimes we use the Scripture passage as a springboard to broaden our prayer for the pastor. Scripture can become a jump-off point to get you started on the right track; then allow the Holy Spirit to amplify and expand the passage to relevant areas that need prayer covering. Notice also how the verses give you insights into what to pray for your pastor. (These verses are actually applicable for anyone, including yourself.)

Heart Preparation

The pastor needs to have a heart that longs to be with God more than anything else. If his heart does not long for God, your pastor will not make time to be with God. The following three verses express similar thoughts, but they have subtle differences that can be prayed to the Lord as different facets of the same theme.

+ *As the deer pants for streams of water, so my soul pants for you, O God. My soul thirsts for God, for the living God. (Psalm 42:1–2)*

Father, help _____ to have a heart that longs for You as a thirsty deer pants for streams of water in a desert place. Help him to cry out to You from the depth of his soul, to need You more than anything or anyone else.

Your pastor needs a growing, deepening relationship with God in prayer. Only as he keeps that close relationship with the Lord will he be able to handle all of the many demands and stresses of his job. And prayer is pivotal to a deepening relationship. Consider these verses and the following prayer:

+ *O God, you are my God, earnestly I seek you; my soul thirsts for you, my body longs for you, in a dry and weary land where there is no water. . . . I stay close to you; your right hand upholds me. (Psalm 63:1,8)*

Father, help our pastor have such a thirst for You in his soul that he longs for You as he would for water in the desert. Make this thirst for You cause him to grow closer in a deepening relationship with You, especially in prayer. May he stay close to You, allowing You to uphold him at all times. Help him to rely on You to uphold him, and not his own abilities.

Right Priority

As already noted, a pastor's time with the Lord needs to be his highest priority. He should not allow other "good" things to squeeze out quality time with his heavenly Father. Sometimes even when his heart is in the right place, he shouldn't let the good become the enemy of the best. Here are two sets of verses and two sample prayers to help in this area of priorities:

+ *One thing I ask of the Lord, this is what I seek: that I may dwell in the house of the Lord all the days of my life, to gaze upon the beauty of the Lord and to seek him in his temple. . . . My heart says of you, "Seek his face!" Your face, Lord, I will seek. (Psalm 27:4, 8)*

Lord, let my pastor spend quality time with You, being with You on a daily basis. Teach him how to enjoy You, to see You in all your beauty and glory, to have a real sense of how wonderful, how awesome You are. Teach him daily new truths about Yourself so in turn he can share with us what You are showing him. Let his heart be quick to respond to whatever You say to him.

+ *"[We] will give our attention to prayer and the ministry of the word."* (Acts 6:4)

Help my pastor to put prayer and the ministry at the forefront of all he does. Help him not to let other things squeeze these vital parts of his life. Show him how to delegate some of these less important responsibilities.

Sensing God's Presence

Ask the Lord to make His presence very real to your pastor during his prayer time. Pray that he will sense God's pleasure in him. Too often the pastor hears about someone's displeasure with him. Here are two Scripture passages and sample prayers to help your pastor in his fellowship with the Father.

+ *"Teach me your ways so I may know you and continue to find favor with you. . . ." The Lord replied, "My Presence will go with you, and I will give you rest."* (Exodus 33:13–14)

Teach our pastor Your ways, Lord, so that he may know You and continue to find favor with You. Show him any time he is straying from Your ways. Help him to listen to You and not to be intimidated by man when Your way differs from what others may advise him. Show him how much You hold him in great favor.

+ *By day the Lord directs his love, at night his song is with me—a prayer to the God of my life.* (Psalm 42:8)

Lord, direct Your love towards our pastor all day long. Let him be keenly aware of Your great love for him. Give him a special song in the night after all his many activities of the day. May his heart rejoice in You.

For the next two verses, why don't you try your hand at composing a prayer based on each. Focus on how special your pastor is to the Lord and on God's heart towards him.

+ *Yet the Lord longs to be gracious to you; he rises to show you compassion.* (Isaiah 30:18)

+ *The Lord your God is with you, he is mighty to save. He will take great delight in you, he will quiet you with his love, he will rejoice over you with singing.* (Zephaniah 3:17)

Other Prayers

Now that you have seen these six samples and done a couple yourself, you should be able to apply the same principles to praying for the following areas from the Scriptures we've suggested. After reading the suggested Scripture passages, pray them back to the Lord.

Having the joy of the Lord. Your pastor's time with the Lord should be a time of refreshing, renewal, expanded perspective, joy, and encouragement, no matter what is going on in his life. He needs to have the joy of the Lord. (Pray through Psalm 16:11; 43:4; Habakkuk 3:17–18.)

Hearing the Lord's voice. The pastor needs to hear clearly from the Lord what His will is and then how to implement it. (Pray through Isaiah 30:21 and Proverbs 3:5–6.)

Being a prayer example. One of the more important things a pastor does is to be a model for his staff as well as the congregation. Therefore, pray for a burden to intercede for and model prayer to his staff, leadership, and congregation. (Pray through 1 Samuel 12:23 and Romans 1:9–10.)

Walking with the Lord

The pastor needs to be strong in several areas in order to walk consistently and strongly with the Lord.

First, *he needs to be devoted to the Word and sound doctrine.* (Pray through Psalm 119:97.)

Second, *he must be Spirit-filled.* This means that he walks under the Spirit's control moment by moment, no matter what is occurring in his life and ministry. (Pray through Galatians 5:16a; Ephesians 5:18b.)

Third, *he needs to grow in faith and trust.* He will have many chances to do this since the pastorate always provides ample growth opportunities. (Pray through Proverbs 3:25–26.)

His Time and Relationship with His Family

The Lord wants the pastor's family relationships to be strong even though he is involved in full-time ministry. In fact, God seems to hold Christian leaders to a higher standard. (See Titus 1:6–9.) The pastor's family is central to who he is and to his emotional well-being; so here are several areas for your prayer focus.

First, *pray that each family member will be loving,* unselfish, respectful, understanding, honoring, and harmonious. (Pray through Ephesians 5:25; 1 Peter 3:7; Ephesians 5:33; 6:1–2.)

Second, *ask that every family member be a source of joy and blessing* to each other. (Pray through Proverbs 20:7; 23:24; 31:28, 30b.)

Third, *pray for protection for all family members,* and that they will enjoy good health, joy, and peace in all circumstances. (Pray through John 14:27; Philippians 4:7.)

A spiritual battle awaits your pastor and his family. As you pray for relationships within the pastor's family, remember that the enemy will often direct special attacks against the family. If Satan can get the pastor's family to be upset, sick, or unhappy, then your pastor will have to take extra time to deal with the results of these attacks. Too often this lessens his effectiveness as a pastor.

Here are three ways you can pray for the family facing spiritual attack. First, *pray for harmony and good health among family members.* Second, *pray for the pastor's wife to feel a part of his ministry and of the church.* That may seem a nonissue, yet a pastor's wife at times may feel offended or alienated by church members. This can happen in three ways. One, members can expect too much from her. Two, she will too often take as a family offense those who oppose her husband. Three, people may expect her children to be perfect because they are the pastor's children. This puts too much pressure on her and them.

Therefore you may also pray that the church will recognize that it called the pastor, not his wife. Pray that your pastor would have the words and sensitivity to make this clear to any who try to take advantage of his wife's time and abilities. You also can ask the Lord to help his wife not feel she has to abstain from all ministry in order not to be taken advantage of; pray that she would want to serve as any other church member would.

Third, *pray that members have reasonable expectations for the pastor's children.* The children may be hurt by the response of church members to them, especially if they are active, normal children.

You need to pray that the church members will not cause hurt to any family member; that they will not expect from pastor's children anything more than they expect from their own children. Then ask the Lord to make the children see ministry as a positive thing and to be proud of their father's work. (Pray through Proverbs 20:7.)

Remember too that this spiritual battle will confront your pastor individually. The Scriptures tell us that Satan roams around like a roaring lion, trying to devour whomever he can (1 Peter 5:8). And pastors are his prime targets. Satan knows that if he can successfully attack the undershepherd, then the sheep will lose their way and/or scatter. Realize, therefore, that your pastor is like a lightning rod for your church. Remember Pastor Roll's devastating experience with his church? His success caused the enemy to jump all over him, trying to keep him from being able to successfully lead the church.

Satan succeeded with Pastor Roll. Don't let that happen in your church! Provide the necessary prayer covering to intercept those fiery darts and shut the lion's mouth. Build a strong prayer hedge of protection around him. Get others to join with you.

No matter how strong your pastor may be or how holy his walk, he needs to have your prayer covering for successfully resisting temptation in two key areas. The first is pride. It is hard sometimes to not get a swelled head when you are successful and people praise you a lot. Humility is God's standard. Satan fell through pride. Ask the Lord to help your pastor always to accept praise with a pure heart and not to think of himself more highly than he should. Ask God to help him not to compare himself or his ministry to anyone else's.

The second area of temptation is sexual—both in actual needs and in his thought life. From the hundreds of pastors we have spoken to or counseled, it appears that a growing number are hooked on pornography and/or TV and video material that is ungodly; others are tempted by these media. Pray that the Lord will keep your pastor pure in all ways, and able to resist whatever temptations the enemy may bring across his path. (Pray through James 4:7; 2 Thessalonians 3:2–3.)

Time Management and Wisdom

With people and projects pulling him from all directions, the pastor must be very wise in how he schedules his day. If he is not careful, the good things may squeeze out the important, even crucial things. He needs to have the mind of the Lord for each day and be willing to let the Lord interrupt him when necessary. He needs discernment to know when an interruption is from the Lord and when it is from another source.

As part of this, pray that the Lord will guard his time and not allow unnecessary interruptions to dominate his time, such as people "dropping in," calling with things that are not appropriate and/or necessary, misplacing things, getting in traffic jams, yes, and even having unexpected church or family emergencies that disrupt his schedule. Ask the Lord to order his time. (Pray Psalm 31:15; Job 14:5.)

It is imperative that your pastor have the mind of the Lord in all he does so that he can rightly lead the church. Yet he will often have several conflicting options from which to choose, especially if influential people in the church are trying to get him to do something the way they want it done. Therefore pray for his discernment, that he might make the right decisions and exercise wisdom in his choices. (Pray 1 Corinthians 2:10–12, 16.)

No Fear of Man, Only of God

Once your pastor has the mind of the Lord, it will be important that he not be afraid of man.

Many pastors have too great a concern for what others think about what they do and say. It is important to take others into consideration, but the pastor needs to first consider what God wants. Once he knows that, he must follow God's leading and let God take responsibility for the reactions of others.

Ask the Lord to give your pastor a healthy fear of Him, and the courage to do all He shows him to do. Pray that he will allow the Lord to fight his battles and show others he is right. Ask for a healthy balance in this area, that there will not be any arrogance, but rather a Spirit-controlled response in love to those who question him when he has followed what the Lord has shown him to do or say. (Pray Psalm 37:5–7a, 23–24; Proverbs 3:5–7; 29:25; Isaiah 26:3–4; 41:10; John 5:30.)

Fruitful Ministry

For a pastor, fruitfulness encompasses a number of areas. He needs to be able to handle with grace and patience his many responsibilities. He needs to develop a sensitivity to the leading of the Lord both as he prepares and as he speaks. He also needs strong, close, harmonious working relationships with staff and leadership. Pray for him to have insights into the solutions for problems and to be able to identify and avoid potential problems.

Ask that he will know how to counsel those who need advice or correction. Above all, everything will need to be done under the control of the Holy Spirit. (Pray through John 15:16; Colossians 1:28.)

A fruitful ministry also means your pastor fulfills his God-given task of equipping his people for ministry. As noted earlier, the pastor is to get his people actively doing the work of the Lord. This means they need to be discipled and then given opportunities to serve. Pray for his discernment to know the gift mix of each person and to challenge church members to use those gifts. Pray that church members will listen and respond to the Spirit's prompting. (Pray through Ephesians 4:11–13; 2 Timothy 2:2.)

HOW TO BLESS YOUR PASTOR

The idea of a *blessing* is the concept of bestowing a gift on someone. The motivating factor for the one doing the blessing is the personal realization that he or she has been blessed both spiritually and temporally by God. There are many ways you can bless your pastor in prayer. It may be in the form of encouragement, prayer, or a tangible gift. You can find verses that talk about the blessed man and claim them for him. Here are a few of our favorites: Psalms 40:4; 84:5; 89:15–17; 112:1; Proverbs 8:34. In these verses notice that often you will bless the pastor by praying specific qualities into his life.

We suggest you pray through each verse on behalf of your pastor. In addition, be on the lookout for other verses you can pray; add them to your list. Your prayers can become a strong weapon in God's hands to strengthen your pastor so that he will truly feel prayed for and not preyed on. Get others to join you. Let him know you are praying for him. Be specific.

The job of the pastor is not an easy one. He doesn't expect it to be. But you can strengthen his heart as you pray for him, as you become his Aaron and Hur in lifting up his hands in the midst of all he does.

Let him know you are praying in depth for him. Drop him a note once in a while telling him of your appreciation of him and how you are praying for some specific things in his life and ministry. You will never know how much that will mean to him, how your words, your note may be used of God to break a current attack of the enemy on him. Be certain; he will hear from almost everyone who is dissatisfied. He needs to hear much more from those who are walking with him, surrounding him with prayer. When he knows you are there for him in such a position of strength, then he will be better able to face all of the criticism, the difficult decisions, the long hours of the ministry.

Now we are ready to look at more ways you can support your pastor.

6

the m&ms
of support

A lot has changed in fifty years. We were both born as baby boomers; we both are pastors; and we both are named Glen (though Glenn spells his name differently, and one of us looks older). From polio vaccine and penicillin to contact lenses and computer chips, we and other baby boomers have seen enormous change in the past half century. (Yes, some baby boomers now are entering their fifties.)

Remember when there were five-and-dime stores, where you bought things for five and ten cents? Now that won't even cover sales tax on most items. As one wit has noted, once for a nickel "you could ride a street car, make a phone call, buy a Pepsi or enough stamps to mail one letter and two postcards." Not anymore!

A lot has changed, hasn't it? But as we approach the subject of pastoral ministry and encouraging your pastor's heart, we remind you of one thing that hasn't changed: the need for support.

THE PASTOR'S RESPONSIBILITY

Your prayers give support, of course, but there are other ways to encourage your pastor's heart. When we consider our pastors' duties, it is clear they need such support.

Paul was often a spokesman for God. In mentoring Timothy, a young pastor, he wrote, "Do the work of an evangelist, discharge all the duties of your ministry" (2 Timothy 4:5). But what are these duties? As pastors we can tell you that the scope of a pastor's responsibilities is huge. Remember the "Responsibility Quotient" you measured in chapter 2, with its fifty-plus points? Most, if not all, of those points fall within the broad scope of most pastors' job descriptions. Those tasks are what man expects. But what does God expect? In Acts 6:4 He narrows it down to two main areas: "Prayer and the ministry of the word." In 1 Timothy 5:17 and 2 Timothy 4:2, Paul emphasized to Timothy that preaching and teaching are key responsibilities of a pastor.

Stop for a minute and think about this: The pastor has a heavy burden because he is to set an example for the believers in godliness. He is to give himself to prayer and the ministry of the Word and to fulfill all the other duties of his ministry. Easy to say, harder to do. Yet, concerning all of these things, Paul makes it even more exacting. "Be diligent in these matters; give yourself wholly to them, so that everyone may see your progress. Watch your life and doctrine closely. Persevere in them, because if you do, you will save both yourself and your hearers" (1 Timothy 4:15–16). Paul recognized that the pastor is in a fishbowl, with his life being scrutinized by everyone. Believe us, this is a heavy burden.

In order to be successful, a pastor must enter the ministry and pursue it through the years with confidence, not a confidence born out of his own merit, education, training, or experience—or even his congregation's compliments—but a confidence that has its roots in a relationship with God. A confidence that comes as a gift from God because of one's calling to God's service.

Such confidence is born of deepest humility. No one has within himself anything to qualify him to serve the Lord's people as a teacher, overseer, and leader. Yet, pastors are called to this very work and they must do it. Paul wrote of how the Christian minister must preach: "We do not preach ourselves, but Jesus Christ as Lord, and ourselves as your servants for Jesus' sake" (2 Corinthians 4:5).

God expects pastors to preach Jesus Christ as Lord and to do so in humility, not drawing attention to themselves (2 Corinthians 10:8; 11:30, Galatians 6:4) nor seeking the approval of men but of God (Galatians 1:10; 1 Thessalonians 2:4).

SUPPORTING THE PASTOR
THROUGH THE "M&MS"

We have identified seven major areas where you can strengthen your pastor's heart. They all begin with the letter *M,* so we call them the M&Ms of support. Don't just read the M&Ms, though. Think about ways you can implement them as part of your lifestyle of ministry.

1. Mission

The call of a pastor is a deeply personal thing. We were both deeply affected when God decided to move us out of other very successful arenas into the field of ministry. But we both readily admit that if it were not for the congregations in which we serve, we would not have experienced the kind of fulfillment that God intended. *Church members can help the pastor focus on that mission* by helping him with secondary tasks wherever possible.

Acts 6 and 8 describe two situations in the life of the early church in which the laity helped the leadership, working as a team with them. These are good examples for us to follow today. In Acts 6, as mentioned earlier, widows within the church were being neglected in the daily distribution of food. The apostles knew that they did not have the time for this nor was this their responsibility. They asked the church to select seven men from the church (Acts 6:3–4). The apostles at that time were the pastors of the Word; they turned over this other responsibility to able men within the church. In Acts 8, a great persecution arose and "all except the apostles were scattered" to other places; and then "those who had been scattered preached the word wherever they went" (Acts 8:1, 4). As a result of the faithful "lay people," the church spread and new churches were established in many cities, including the great early church in Antioch from which Paul was sent forth as a missionary.

Whether ministering to the widows in the church or witnessing to nonbelievers, the example set for us in Acts was that the early "pastors" continued in prayer and the ministry of the Word while other faithful men and women in the church did the other work. On occasions the apostles ministered to widows and evangelized the lost, but most of their time was spent in the ministry of the Word and prayer. That was most necessary in order to equip and enable the rest of the church to be effective in the use of their gifts and service.

Clearly the shepherds of the church have a distinct mission as they prepare the rest of the saints for service to God. We can help by letting them do their primary task, assisting them with the secondary tasks whenever possible. We do so by using our gifts. (See point three, below.)

2. Money

We all have experienced at times the pressures that finances can put on our emotional and physical well-being. Finances can distract us so much that we can feel almost paralyzed or at least become marginalized in our abilities to cope with underfinancing. This is also true in a pastor's life or in the ministry.

Therefore, the second way you can support your pastor is *to give generously to the church budget and to see that the church gives generous financial support to him*. While there have been cases of financial abuses by pastors, we must not paint all pastors with the same brush. The vast majority of the pastors in this country are truly men of God, called, gifted, equipped, and passionate about the ministry. It grieves us that many appear to be so undervalued and underpaid. We cannot help but believe that this is not pleasing to God.

Paul wrote Timothy to instruct the churches in this way, "The elders who direct the affairs of the church well are worthy of double honor, especially those whose work is preaching and teaching. For the Scripture says, 'Do not muzzle the ox while it is treading out the grain,' and 'The worker deserves his wages'" (1 Timothy 5:17–18). As you can see, God's Word mandates that the church must provide the livelihood for those elders who spend their time in the ministry of the Word and prayer. In most churches this individual is called the pastor. The requirement is that some material benefit be given to that person by the church, but it is not a matter of reward for work well done. It is a matter of providing for his needs while he is engaged in that work.

Paul deals at more length with this subject in 1 Corinthians 9:7–11, 13–14. He concludes in verse 11 with a rhetorical question:

"If we have sown spiritual seed among you, is it too much if we reap a material harvest from you?" Clearly it is not. Three verses later he asks another question to emphasize the need to financially support the church leader: "Don't you know that those who work in the temple get their food from the temple, and those who serve at the altar share in what is offered on the altar? In the same way, the Lord has commanded that those who preach the gospel should receive their living from the gospel" (vv. 13–14). Please notice he does not say "existence." It is to be a wage to live on, one that is to provide for all his needs since for most pastors this is their only major source of income.

We realize that some churches are not large enough to provide a full-time salary for their pastors. But in such instances, the church needs to allow him the time to take an outside job to supplement his income so he can provide properly for his family.

Several factors should influence how much to pay. Some pastors need more than others to live on, for instance those with large families. Pastors with more education and more experience and those who have been at the church for many years, proving themselves, perhaps should receive greater remuneration than others, but the principle of the Scriptures is the same for everyone. Each church should provide as generously as possible for its pastor so that his time may be given as fully as possible to his ministry in that church.

This is not an area to see how much savings the church can get away with. It brings shame and disgrace on the name of the Lord when pastors have to scrimp in order to make ends meet. Too often it is the family members that suffer, either from lack, or from the wife having to get a job when she is desperately needed at home both for her children and for her husband.

3. Ministry

If you want your pastor to be the best pastor you have ever had, you must do your part as a member of the church. First, you must understand your own importance in the body; you have a specific and vital part in the spiritual health and proper functioning of the church. God has given you gifts and has called you to some work within the church. He needs you to faithfully carry out that work.

The Lord needs you, the church needs you, and your pastor needs you.

Second, determine your spiritual gifts if you haven't already. Use the following abbreviated checklist to help learn your spiritual gift(s) and natural abilities. The list is not exhaustive and the second one is not specifically spiritual gifts, but rather skills or training, special talents you may have been given or may have acquired that should be used in the Lord's service and for the work of the church.

We can determine our spiritual gifts through prayer, aptitude, and input from others. Before you check any of these items, pray, asking for God's guidance, and also consider past experiences in any of these areas; were your experiences positive? Those may be signs of aptitude. Consider taking a spiritual gifts inventory that may be available at your church. You also could read a book on recognizing your gifts. (See text below.) To determine your natural talents and abilities, consider past positive experiences and your own interest or enjoyment of any of these as indicators of your abilities.

HEARTBEATS
Partial Checklist for
Spiritual Gifts and Natural Abilities

SPIRITUAL GIFTS

Check any that apply.

☐ Word of Wisdom   ☐ Hospitality

☐ Word of Knowledge   ☐ Teaching

☐ Faith   ☐ Encouragement

☐ Gifts of Healing   ☐ Giving

☐ Prophecy   ☐ Leadership

☐ Service   ☐ Mercy

NATURAL TALENTS AND ABILITIES

Identify your talents and abilities.

- ☐ Music
- ☐ Art
- ☐ Writing

- ☐ Drama
- ☐ Maintenance/mechanical skills
- ☐ Administrative (bookkeeping, secretarial, etc.)

Many excellent books discuss the gifts of the Holy Spirit. We encourage you to find one or more that are in line with your particular theological perspective, especially those that may include questionnaires or inventories to determine your gift or gifts. In *Your Spiritual Gifts Can Help Your Church Grow,* for example, C. Peter Wagner includes a 125-item questionnaire which helps the reader to identify his or her spiritual gift(s). He also has a five-step process for growing through using spiritual gifts.

Two other good books are *Discover Your Spiritual Gift and Use It* and *Finding and Using Your Spiritual Gifts,* by Rick Yohn and Tim Blanchard, respectively. Blanchard's book contains a Spiritual Gifts Inventory Questionnaire along with some excellent evaluation tools, including how to evaluate preferences and tendencies, your past Christian service experiences, and yourself against each gift. Once you have identified your gifting, he then has a list of different church activities a person with such a gift would be qualified to do.

Third, take the initiative, volunteering to put your gift to work in the church. After you have determined what gifts and abilities you have, Paul's advice to Timothy is good advice for you, "Do not neglect your gift and fan into flame the gift of God" (2 Timothy 1:6, author paraphrase). It's as important for you as it is for your pastor to use every gift, skill, and bit of experience in the Lord's work. The neglect of any gift will hurt the church and deprive it of an essential part of its ministry. To neglect our own gifts will hurt us and deprive us of the joys of faithful and full service to the Lord and to His church. Your pastor needs you to be one of those reliable men or women to whom he can entrust the work of the church. He needs you to express your desire to use your gifts fully and to serve as a leader in the church. True, he may, in time, discover that you could be such a person, but if you tell him now, much time can be saved in preparing you for whatever work you are going to do.

But we can almost hear some of you saying, "This challenge may be good and well for those who are talented, but I don't have any special gifts. What am I suppose to do?" The work of the church should be done by every member doing his own part, exercising his own gifts. Your gift may not be a public gift easily put on display, but whatever gift you have received is special, bestowed by the Holy Spirit. The work of the church should be done in the same way a body functions so that the whole church is a coordinated unit (one body) with many different members doing their proper work in their own way. Your work properly and faithfully done will enable and encourage your pastor to do his work and to become the best pastor you ever had.

If you already are involved in some part of the church's ministry, you know the rewards (and occasional challenges) of service to God through His local church. Perhaps your pastor is already aware of your leadership in the church. But he still needs you to tell him, "I will do everything I can to help you and the ministry of the church, to work with you, and to do my part faithfully." He needs to hear that from you.

4. Mind

Vital to the well-being and support of any leader are ample opportunities to learn and expand his knowledge base. We both have spent a good portion of our adult life in what would be called continuing education. The reason is not because we are pseudo-intellectuals (which means we've been educated beyond our level of intelligence), but rather because we want to stay current, stimulated, challenged, and continually pushed to pursue excellence in life and ministry. We don't always seek training just in the areas of theology and pastoral ministry. Other areas of personal interest and hobbies have helped to fuel our creativity.

A church membership that desires to support their pastor will take a portion of their budget to provide for continuing education expenses. In the final chapter we will give several specific ideas for helping your pastor grow professionally; many go beyond the formal classroom setting. Of course, helping your pastor complete graduate studies or take specific professional courses is always appropriate. Keep in mind that the key to any policy should be creativity and flexibility.

5. Management

Pastors have good hearts and love their people. They often try to do everything, but if a pastor attempts to spread out his efforts to things he has no gifting for and no particular interest in, he will be in trouble. He will find himself doing such things as a matter of duty with no love for it. He too often will become so frustrated about having to do so many things for which he is unqualified or feels inadequate that by the time he gets to the important things—say his sermon preparation or prayer—he has been drained by the lesser activities.

We all know from firsthand experience the close connection between our mental and physical states. Pastors are very human. Therefore, they, too, can be impaired by having to do something that drains their energies. Overload a pastor and he will do little good there and will only hurt his ministry and the ministry of the church. But if he knows his gifts and uses them in his ministry and pursues those ministries for which he is gifted, he will be a good pastor, wisely using his time and effectively ministering to those under his care. We all want our churches to run well. And no one wants this more than the pastor.

Yet amazingly enough, we sometimes so unreasonably overload the pastor that we make this goal unobtainable. Remember, the pastor must give part of his time to meeting with boards, committees, and an occasional task force. He must keep communication open through bulletins, newsletters, and other means of publicity and information. He writes letters, sends out mailings, and makes phone calls. All of this administrative work is important for the shepherd to lead the church in the right direction.

So what is God's solution to this major workload? Teamwork!

Because it is humanly impossible for a pastor to do everything, he has the responsibility to train others in the church to do the works for which they are gifted (2 Timothy 2:2; though Paul cited teaching, instruction should extend to all areas of church ministry).

A beautiful cooperation can develop between a pastor and the church family. The pastor can provide suitable resources for various members to work in the church in the area of their giftedness. After all, he knows that he is the servant of God and the church, and that his job is not to make all the decisions and to run the church. But, decisions have to be made. Your pastor sees the need, and he will do the work if no one else will. Don't put him in that position. Accept a spot on one of the committees or boards; offer to help put out the newsletter or the bulletin. Tell him you are an artist and would be glad to help prepare publicity for special events. Tell him you are a good secretary and would be glad to spend three hours a week to help out in the office. Tell him you are handy with fixing things, cleaning up, painting, or any one of the dozens of jobs that need doing around your church.

Maybe a retired businessman can volunteer or work part time in the areas of administration. Just don't allow your pastor to labor under the weight of tasks that others can do. When the laity helps in such areas, the pastor can focus on the more important work of preaching and ministering to people.

6. Meditation

It's a basic rule of life: something in motion uses up energy and that energy source has to be replenished. For instance, we eat and sleep to replenish the energy that we used up during the day. Our cars have to be refueled because you can go only so far on a tank of gas. The same is true of the pastor. Many clergy work and minister long hours each week. They give of themselves, physically, emotionally, and spiritually.

Provide your pastor with the necessary (maybe even mandatory) refueling time. A friend of ours was being installed as the new pastor of a church in the northeast. During the section known as the "charge to the congregation," the speaker made this statement: "Protect your pastor's private time. For instance, if you're planning on dying soon, please don't do it on a Monday." While not everyone was captivated by his sense of humor, he did get his point across: Pastors need time to refuel.

7. Marriage and Family

Most congregations do not realize the stress placed upon the pastoral family. One pastor recounted the following story as he was trying to protect his family from this stress. Evidently his youngest son came running down the center aisle of the sanctuary one Wednesday night during a prayer meeting. One of the "mature saints" shared just loud enough for everyone to hear, "Look at the pastor's son running in the sanctuary." The pastor, recognizing that this was a teaching moment, vital to the welfare of his family, shared, "Dear friends, you know he's the pastor's son, I know he's the pastor's son, but please don't let him know he's the pastor's son." That pastor wanted his congregation to know his boy did not deserve special, favored treatment or special, condemning judgment.

Being a pastor's wife can be equally challenging. Many churches feel that by hiring the pastor they get the wife as a bonus, expecting her to play an instrument, sing on demand, lead the choir, head up committees, and spearhead all new innovations in children's ministry. But she may not have spiritual gifts or natural talents in those areas. Great expectations affect not just the pastor, but often his spouse as well.

The issue of supporting the pastor and family and helping to strengthen the husband and wife's marriage is so important that we will return to the topic in depth in the two final chapters. There we will address problems of various spiritual temptations as well as offer several suggestions for supporting the pastor's family.

OUR *PERSONAL* SUPPORT

During the 1994 Olympic Games in Atlanta, our friend Jim Neal and his wife had the opportunity to attend several events. At one of the track and field events, they took the time to enjoy the sport of people-watching. Literally thousands were in the stands. They observed a young girl from Jews for Jesus near an aisle entrance, passing out tracts to anyone who would accept them. Then Jim noticed many people standing and sitting in that same area—some of them alone. He wondered whether a more effective and efficient witness would be for the girl to simply sit down next to some of those people for one-on-one discussions. As he turned to tell his wife about this enlightened idea, Jim suddenly noticed that the young girl had entered into a conversation with a woman walking toward her seat—except the girl had to write her side of the conversation since she was not able to talk.

How easy it is for us to stand on the sidelines and suggest better ways for others to carry out the work of Christ. The most important thing is that we become involved, supporting our pastor in tangible ways.

7

positive participation

There was once a small jazz club in New Orleans. In a corner of that club sat an old dilapidated piano. All of the jazz artists complained about this antiquated instrument and how poor their music sounded. The piano players dreaded playing on it. The vocalists dreaded singing with it. And every combo that played at the club, without exception, wished they could bring in their own piano—just like they would bring their own saxophone or trumpet. Finally after years of listening to these jazz musicians complain about his piano, the owner of the club decided to do something about it. He had the piano painted.[1]

It seems ridiculous that someone would try to change a piano's sound by painting it—that's not getting at the root cause. But similarly Christians sometimes come to church and don't want to deal with root causes to bring about change in their lives. Pastors know members of the congregation who simply nod their heads in agreement but never allow the messages to penetrate their lives. They would have been satisfied with a painted piano; they may never take the steps necessary to make fundamental changes in their lives because they are unwilling to learn from their shepherd's instruction.

WHAT GOD EXPECTS

During the early days of the church, the apostles asked the church to appoint seven men who could direct a certain ministry within the church, a ministry of service to the widows. The instructions were: "Choose seven men from among you who are known to be full of the Spirit and wisdom. We will turn this responsibility over to them and will give our attention to prayer and the ministry of the word" (Acts 6:3–4). The ministry of the Word and prayer has remained the foundation of the pastoral ministry.

Hear Preaching and Teaching

The Scriptures are clear that the pastor is to preach and teach the Word of God and his flock is to hear and heed it. At most ordination services, Paul's charge to Timothy is read. It is a solemn and sacred charge:

+ *In the presence of God and of Christ Jesus, who will judge the living and the dead, and in view of his appearing and his kingdom, I give you this charge: Preach the Word; be prepared in season and out of season; correct, rebuke and encourage—with great patience and careful instruction.* (2 Timothy 4:1–2)

Paul then added that this task of teaching would become difficult because people would listen only to what they wanted to hear. Then he finished the charge with these words: "Keep your head in all situations, endure hardship, do the work of an evangelist, discharge all the duties of your ministry" (verse 5).

The basic work of your pastor is to preach and teach the Word of God. "Devote yourself to the public reading of Scripture, to preaching and to teaching," Paul advised Timothy (1 Timothy 4:13). Why is this work so important? Because "all Scripture is God-breathed and is useful for teaching, rebuking, correcting and training in righteousness, so that the man of God may be thoroughly equipped for every good work" (2 Timothy 3:16–17). Every Christian needs to be equipped for every good work, and that is done through the teaching of the Word of God. It cannot be done without it.

Have Changed Lives

The goal of such preaching is to present every man perfect in Christ. Changed lives, complete and mature in Christ, is the goal. In fact, in all pastoral ministry, the pastor struggles to this end, with all the power and wisdom that God gives. And a pastor cannot hope to present anyone perfect or complete in Christ unless he proclaims Christ and teaches the Word of God. *Faith* comes by hearing the Word (Romans 10:17). *Knowledge* comes from the Word. *Wisdom* comes from the Word. *We overcome temptations* by the Word of God (see Matthew 4 and Ephesians 6). *Our spiritual strength and wisdom come from the Word, so the teaching of that Word to one's people becomes the basic necessity of pastoral ministry.*

The biblical admonition is vital for your pastor: "Do your best to present yourself to God as one approved, a workman who does not need to be ashamed and who correctly handles the word of truth" (2 Timothy 2:15).

ESSENTIAL NEEDS OF ANY PASTOR

Remember, an effective pastor is one who preaches for change. He wants to change you. The biblical mandate is to preach the Word and prepare the flock to correctly handle that Word. For your pastor to do this, he needs to prepare. He needs time—time (1) to study, (2) to meditate, and (3) to labor in the Word. He also needs privacy and uninterrupted hours to spend digging out of the Word all those treasures that both he and his people need.

His sermons are not to be the eloquent rhetoric of a trained speaker, but the thoughts and words of God being spoken by God's proclaimer of truth. To be ready for such a ministry, the pastor needs hours each week to spend in prayer, meditation, and study of God's Word.

To Guard His Trust

Your pastor has a sacred trust. "He must hold firmly to the trustworthy message as it has been taught, so that he can encourage others by sound doctrine and refute those who oppose it" (Titus 1:9). This is essential: Your pastor is to "guard what has been entrusted to [his] care," and he is to keep "the pattern of sound teaching" which he has in the Scriptures (1 Timothy 6:20; 2 Timothy 1:13). He is responsible to God for this trust; he cannot spend his time in other things to the neglect of this work. He is not to spend his time exclusively in his study, certainly, but he cannot spend so much time away from his study or attending to other things in his study that he fails to fully satisfy God's expectations in the ministry of teaching.

To Exercise Proper Authority

Note that in his charge to Timothy, Paul wrote to "correct, rebuke and encourage—with great patience and careful instruction." Titus was told to "encourage and rebuke with all authority" (Titus 2:15). Thus the pastor has the authority of God's Word to rebuke and correct as well as to encourage. Yet many pastors spend much time trying to encourage the people but very little time correcting and rebuking with authority.

He has the authority of his office as an overseer and elder within the church. Significantly, he has the "authority the Lord gave us for building you up rather than pulling you down" (2 Corinthians 10:8). *It is the authority of love, not of a tyrant but of a father for his children.* It is the authority that is given to those who have responsibility for the welfare of another.

Such authority is appropriate for your pastor to have, but he must use it in an appropriate manner. *He must be gentle, compassionate, and humble, yet firm and uncompromising in the things of God.* If the Scripture is clear in its demands, and we believe it is, then the pastor must be clear in explaining those demands and insistent that God's people carry out those demands to the fullest.

In using his authority, the pastor needs to heed Paul's admonition that "the Lord's servant must not quarrel; instead, he must be kind to everyone, able to teach, not resentful. Those who oppose him he must gently instruct, in the hope that God will grant them repentance leading them to a knowledge of the truth, and that they will come to their senses and escape from the trap of the devil, who has taken them captive to do his will" (2 Timothy 2:24–25). He must not be arrogant or abusive or abrasive in his attitude towards those who differ from him. When disagreements arise, he must avoid arguments and controversies. (See Titus 3:9–11.)

To Teach the Word

The pastor is first of all a teacher. He must labor diligently in the Word, always be prepared to preach the Word, correcting, rebuking, and encouraging with all authority. But if this is a great privilege, it is also a serious responsibility. James wrote, "Not many of you should presume to be teachers, my brothers, because you know that we who teach will be judged more strictly" (James 3:1). So let every pastor use his authority in utmost humility, knowing that whatever he may correct or rebuke in another will be judged first and harshest in his own life. Let him remember that whatever he teaches, he must also seek to practice. What he would require of others under the Word, he must first do himself.

How can you help your pastor be a better teacher? First, you can learn from his teaching. Second, *let him know that you are learning* from him. If you are not learning, find out why. Examine yourself first, however. Here are several questions you can ask yourself as a learner:

1. Do I have a desire to learn more about what the Bible teaches?
2. Do I study the Bible regularly on my own?
3. Do I follow along in my Bible whenever the pastor is preaching and teaching?
4. Do I take notes about what is said so I can study and recall it later?
5. Do I enter church prepared to listen carefully to all that is said so that God can speak to me from His Word?

If you are going to learn from your pastor's teaching, you must do your part. We are participants, not spectators. Students who go to school and sit idly through a class and never open a book or study at home can't expect to learn much from their teacher. They might have a good teacher, yet the teacher cannot teach those who are not ready to learn. The same things apply to your pastor's teaching. We must be students—we listen carefully, take notes, compare the text (Bible), and do our homework (study Scriptures, apply them, and pray). Such students will learn regardless of how good the teacher is.

(See the "Heartbeats" on the next page entitled "How to Hear a Sermon" for guidelines on focusing on a message.)

Perhaps we need to distinguish between going to hear the preacher and going to hear the preaching. If your pastor has studied diligently in the Word and proclaims the Word, you can learn from his preaching, for it is the preaching of the Word. He may or may not be the most eloquent, best-trained, or most dynamic preacher you have ever heard, but if he is preaching the Word, you can learn from the preaching. It is the faithful preaching of the Word that we need, and not necessarily great preachers. *Great preachers are few, but good preaching of the Word can be heard in every pulpit if both pastor and people work hard to have it.*

If your pastor preaches the Word, he will encourage you, but he will also at times correct and rebuke you with authority. If you accept the correction and the rebuke with the same eagerness with which you accept the encouragement, you will learn much from your pastor's teaching.

As you listen and seek to apply the teaching, remember all teaching is valuable. Your pastor is also responsible for *teaching you the great doctrines of the faith.* Listen to them as eagerly as you listen to sermons on daily living and more practical matters. He also is responsible for *teaching you the whole of the Scriptures,* both Old and New Testaments, prophecy, practical living, spiritual victory, and every other subject. Some will seem to be of more benefit and interest at the time, but all of them are necessary to your spiritual welfare.

As you learn, remember that the lessons come outside the sermon as well; not all of your pastor's teaching is done from the pulpit. Some of it is done in various board and committee meetings, Sunday school classes, youth gatherings, private conversations, personal visits. A large portion of his teaching will be done on an individual level. That's where it is the hardest, especially if it is a matter of correction or rebuke. Yet his authority is still in effect, in or out of the pulpit. If you have a position of trust and responsibility in the church, perhaps as a teacher, a deacon, an elder, an officer, and if you are not living right or if you are neglecting your work, your pastor has the responsibility and the authority to speak to you about it. It is a matter of his teaching ministry. He doesn't want to condemn or

---

HEARTBEATS

HOW TO HEAR A SERMON

Listening to a sermon requires proper preparation and attentiveness. Notice that the first three steps are *preparation* before you sit in the pew.

1. Pray that the Lord will remove the debris of the week from your heart. (Colossians 3:1–2)
2. Dismantle any resistance to the Word of God.
   - Deal with any anger. (Ephesians 4:31)
   - Deal with any distractions. (Matthew 13:22)
   - Deal with disbelief. (John 1:11)
3. Seek forgiveness from people you have offended. (Matthew 5:23–24)
4. Give full attention to the Word. (John 5:39)
   - Take notes as the Lord speaks to you.
   - Water the Word with prayer.
   - Seek to share what you have heard with someone else.
5. Live in the light of God's Word. (James 1:22)

---

criticize; he wants to help and encourage. Let him encourage you by helping you do what is right.

A FEAST . . . OR BURNT TOAST

To understand the relationship between the pastor and church family, let's meet Julie and her family. (The parallels will be clear shortly.)

Julie was excited. The mother of three children, she loved cooking and trying out new recipes. A few weeks ago she decided to surprise her family with some new dishes she had found while going through some of her cookbooks. She found the perfect entree, and after some time of looking, identified just the right recipes for complementary vegetables, potatoes, and dessert. She planned out each detail of this special meal for her family, not because it was a special occasion, but rather because of her love for her husband and children. She had to go to two different specialty stores to find just the right ingredients for some of the recipes.

The Special Meal

On the day of the special meal she rose early, knowing she would need extra time not usually available in her normal busy day's schedule. Though she awoke early and had much to do, she loved each part of the preparation, even when at one point she couldn't get the pastry to quite do what she wanted. Her quick call to the cooking expert of the local newspaper provided the solution.

As she put the final touch on the dinner—the extra garnish of paprika sprinkled in an appealing pattern—her heart sang. She anticipated the looks of pleasure and satisfaction on her family's faces as they saw the wonderful meal emerge from the oven. She even made certain, in her roundabout way, that each one would be there for dinner.

Finally, the dinner hour came. Julie carefully set the table, arranging things "just so," and lit the candles. *Here they come!* And she was not disappointed. The unanimous verbal applause from each family member was great reward for the many hours it took to prepare the meal. That night as she reflected on the successful day, she was already planning for the next great meal. Her heart was full of joy and satisfaction in having done a good job and in the way she knew her gift of love had been important to each family member. Life was good. God was good.

Striking Parallels

Julie's experience has many parallels to that of pastors. Our pastors spend long hours to prepare a feast for us each Sunday morning. They have waited on the Lord to get the right "recipe," and then have gone through the "stores" of books to get just the right combination. Unlike Julie, they have consulted many times with the head "Chef" throughout the preparation of the "meal" to know that they have just the right ingredients, the best seasoning for each part, and have spent the necessary time in thorough preparation to give their beloved family a feast. They have a joy in their preparation, doing it in a way that shows the great responsibility they feel towards their church families. The pastor/chef seeks to serve only the best spiritual food, well-prepared and well-presented.

Truly they have poured themselves into the project. For indeed, each sermon is a type of project, a masterly crafted gift God gives His people through His servants, the pastors.

Sunday arrives, the pastors are all prepared, their hearts anticipating the joy others will have as they receive the God-superintended meal. The pastor brings forth each perfectly prepared course and sets it before his church family.

How is it received? The responses vary:

- Some love it and eat their fill. They are overflowing with satisfaction and are very pleased with their spiritual chef.
- Some devour with no thanks.
- Some turn up their noses, saying they've had better cooks.
- Some tell the pastor about different ingredients he should have used.
- Some tell him it was undercooked while others say it was overcooked.
- Still others come so late for the meal that they miss the first part of it.
- Some are so distracted during the meal that they just dabble in giving their attention to the food, missing most of the nutritional parts.

Everyone seems to think they should tell the "spiritual chef" what to prepare, how to do it, and that it should only be done a certain way. Each feels a responsibility to "teach," "help," or "instruct" the spiritual chef in seeing the need to do whatever it is the person determines needs changing.

Now is there anything wrong with this last scenario? Aren't we to encourage others to improve, point out to them their mistakes, and in general help them be the best they can be? Before we address the answer to these oft-voiced questions, let's draw another parallel with Julie's situation.

What would Julie have felt like if her husband always ate his meal, but pointed out some area in which she failed? Or he told her there is dust on the coffee table or a spider web in the corner that has been there for weeks? Her pink candle made him feel like a sissy. A yellow or blue one would have been better, in his estimation. How would her heart feel after such "loving criticism" day in and day out? Would she want to put in the effort? Would she rejoice at his return in the evening? Would she feel awkward in any new attempts to do things for him? Would her actions start stemming from trying to please one who can never be pleased and end up frustrating her, depressing her, stealing her joy?

What if some of the members came late for the meal, gobbled it up without acknowledging how good it was ("After all, isn't this what mothers are for, to fix my meal? Why should I say 'thanks' when she always is cooking for me?"). Or what if they just don't show up and when they finally come home one or two days later, act as though nothing unusual has happened? How would she feel if she fed them things she knew were essential for their health, and they refused to eat it and accused her of not showing love by serving such unwanted food?

Unfortunately, those parallels are all too close to what happens to many a sincere, good pastor who has one or more well-meaning critics or unthinking people in his congregation.

As pastors and ones who work with and counsel many other pastors, we can tell you that most pastors, especially early in their careers, come each Sunday to the pulpit, full of enthusiasm and expectation for how God is going to use that day's sermon. Already they will have benefited from insights He will have been giving them. The minister knows of several message elements that should "hit the spot" in the hearts of specific church family members and meet their spiritual needs or current hunger.

Unfortunately, some of those most "hungry" individuals too often turn up their nose at the presentation or have other excuses why they should not eat the spiritual food in the way it is presented. Such hungry people allow the gremlins of criticism to trick them into rejecting what is offered. And because of our humanity, we who are pastors can be adversely affected by unjust criticism and become "gun-shy" in giving the full counsel of God. Or we become too concerned about how what we will share will be received by our congregation, especially those individuals who have been critical in the past. If we are not careful, our confidence, our joy can slip away, and the whole reason we answered God's call to be an undershepherd can get blurred and distorted as we see our ministry through the distorted eyes and words of certain of our church family members. This is not the way it is supposed to be, but believe us, it all too often is the way it plays out in real life.

A Recipe for Unhappiness

The bottom line, then, is that what we have here is a recipe for unhappiness: unhappiness in the pastor who can't satisfy those he tries to feed, no matter how much he tries or how good the presentation is. He will always have his distracters.

The saddest result of such a scenario is that it can end with a once-good pastor becoming a passive pastor who has lost his fire and vision or even becoming so discouraged by critical church members that he gives up the pastorate. Many pastors we counsel are seriously considering giving up because of the struggles with their flock. They feel beaten up, unloved, unappreciated, and overworked. They are convinced they can never please everyone and that nothing they do will ever fully satisfy their church family. How sad that the enemy can use the church members to be part of removing one God has called to the front lines of His battle! (We will look at his role shortly.)

But it doesn't have to stay this way—it *must not* stay this way—if we are to do things the way God has set them up for the healthy church body. So let's look at some practical ways we can avoid the enemy's trap of being used in a critical or unthinking way against our pastor.

RECOGNIZING THE SOURCE OF YOUR NEGATIVE INPUT

First, let's consider the source of our critical attitudes. Ask yourself the following series of questions in order to better evaluate where any negative thoughts you have come from.

1. Is this something that Jesus thinks about my pastor?
2. Is this a core issue that must be addressed out loud, or is it instead simply something I want because of my own preferences?
3. Is this something that prayer could change without my mentioning it to anyone?
4. What biblical grounds do I have to speak to my spiritual leader—my pastor—about this in light of Matthew 7:1–2 and 1 Corinthians 2:15? (In answering this question, also ask yourself if what you have to say is so important it nullifies these two strong biblical precedents.)
5. If I feel I must speak out on this, have I first prayed about it and gotten the Lord's permission to say something about this?
6. How would I feel if our roles were reversed in this situation and it was I who would hear from my pastor the words I am thinking of saying?

Remember, Satan wishes to tear down the church any way he can. As the accuser of the brethren, he will even use well-meaning believers to attack pastors. He wins in two ways when he uses other believers in his schemes. First, he sends his poisonous darts at the pastor. Any that touch him usually have some impact, even though they may be dealt with right away by the pastor. The unnecessary wound will still be there and have to heal. This steals from him both physical and mental strength. Second, whoever the enemy can get to join him as his mouthpiece of being an accuser is caught in his trap and suffers accordingly.

What are some of the symptoms of one who is caught in an enemy trap? Discontent, dissatisfaction with one or more things, a critical spirit, unrest, turmoil, lack of true peace, the feeling of needing to be on guard with other believers, to be certain the pastor is "pure in doctrine" and doing things the "right" way. When we as churchgoers are unable to really receive much from the sermon since so much time is spent in analysis and evaluation, we must ask, "What is the source?" We must be careful that our hearts are not closed to any working of the Spirit of God.

Please note, however, that we are not saying pastors don't want or need feedback. They do. But it needs to be done sensitively, in love, and at the appropriate time. For example, it is unwise to tell a pastor right after his first message, when he is going to give the same message two or more times, about a perceived error or your different point of view. This can be very deflating to his emotional level and interfere with his subsequent presentation(s). Don't let the enemy use you as a weapon to distract or discourage him.

WAYS TO ENCOURAGE A MINISTER'S PREACHING

Here are five ways you can encourage your pastor in his ministry of preaching the Word of God:

- Pray for him. Let him know you are praying. Find out from him any requests he may have.

- Drop him a note once in a while, mentioning things he has said or done that have been meaningful to you. Mention specifics of how his messages have ministered to you. Where appropriate, mention things about his family members that you've noticed that are positive. (Kids behave well, wife sings/plays piano well, she was a help to a particular person in need, etc.) Ask the Lord to show you ways and things to compliment. Make your comments sincerely, without flattery.

- Remember with at least a card, special days for the pastor and his family members, such as birthdays and anniversaries.

- Mention to special interest groups within the church, especially those of which you are a part, about encouraging the pastor and his family.

- Ask the Lord to show you different, innovative ways to encourage him.

"HOW AM I DOING?"

To measure your participation in these areas, ask yourself the following questions:

99

1. How am I encouraging the pastor each Sunday? During the week?
2. What can I start doing that I have not done in the past to encourage him? How much do I pray for him?
3. If he has a list of those who are behind him and those who are against him, which list should I be on? Why?
4. From my interaction with him, which list am I likely to be on?

So how are you doing? Are you appreciating your pastor and what the Lord is giving him? Are you a positive part of the church family life? If you can answer yes to these questions, then you will be able to learn from your pastor's teaching. That doesn't mean you are to accept blindly everything he has to say. The Berean church was commended for examining the Scriptures every day "to see if what Paul said was true" (Acts 17:11). Paul wrote to the Thessalonians to "test everything" (1 Thessalonians 5:21). Listen carefully to all that he teaches. Examine the Scriptures and put his teaching to the test. See if what he is saying is true, but be careful to test it against the Scriptures themselves and not just the interpretation of the Scriptures that you may have been taught.

If perhaps you have some questions about your pastor's teaching, ask him for a list of Scriptures, and study them carefully, with an open mind. Discuss the interpretation with your pastor honestly and fairly and then allow the Holy Spirit to guide you and teach you the truth. Be prepared for honest differences of opinion about the meanings of some Scriptures. After you have done all of this, you may still not agree. But, if it is not a matter of salvation or essential doctrine, don't let it hinder your fellowship with your pastor. And don't let it keep you from learning from the rest of his teaching.

You want your pastor to be the best pastor you ever had. His basic ministry is in preaching and teaching. Encourage him in that. Allow him time and privacy to prepare for that. Listen carefully and eagerly to all he has to say, both in the pulpit and in private. Test what he says by the Scriptures. Don't resist his authority but let him encourage, correct, and rebuke. Learn from your pastor's teaching. As part of that, work on being a better listener.

8

biblical teamwork

Listen to an orchestra tuning up—sheer chaos to the ear. Each member chooses what to play during the warm-up time. No one is in charge, except perhaps for the lead violinist who gives the initial note for everyone to match. Yes, these are skilled musicians, but nobody is making beautiful music. Each is doing his own thing, his own way. There isn't even unity among the same instruments.

Then a wonderful thing happens. Onto the stage steps the conductor. The audience applauds. Silence, and the conductor raises his baton in authority. Suddenly instruments that have been clashing with each other start producing great music, all in perfect synchronization, with great feeling and interpretation. The musical score for one instrument complements that of every other to produce a symphonic masterpiece that stirs the audience.

What is so special about this man waving the baton? Admittedly, he had training, knew the music well, and had a passion and vision for what he wanted to hear from each instrument. But could he play each instrument? Probably not and certainly not as well as those sitting in front of him. What gave him the right to lead? Authority. An authority from the owner of the orchestra and the conscious submission of even the greatest virtuoso in the group to come under the leadership of this man. They became a team with one goal in mind: to play the same music, at the same tempo, in the same key, with the greatest skill possible as directed by their leader.

Churches are much like orchestras when it comes to teamwork. When operating correctly they have one leader who helps each member contribute his or her part at the right time and in the right way in order to produce the best sound. Just think for a minute of what would happen if just one person, say a temperamental first violinist, decided in the middle of the performance to launch out into his own rendition of the music—maybe even a better one than the conductor was able to produce. No matter how brilliant the violinist, he would be wrong and would mar or even destroy the beauty of what was being produced. Any one or more of the musicians could have the same devastating effect by deciding to play in a different key, at a different tempo, or to improvise without checking it out first; or choose to join in two beats late. What if several got together, were disgruntled and chose to "do it their way?" You get the picture. Chaos! Disharmony!

This is the very reason Jesus prays in John 17 for there to be unity in the church, that we would be one. Not that we would all look alike, speak alike, or minister the same way. But that when we do speak or minister, we would not clash with others; that we would contribute to the "song of the church" rather than be in disharmony. Biblical teamwork is at the center of producing such harmony in our churches.

So what kinds of "dissonant notes" do we hear in the church? They come in all different shapes and sounds. It may be members in hot debate over which translation of the Bible to use, a tense discussion over what kind of building improvement should be next on the agenda, or even a disputed decision on what music to choose—traditional or contemporary—for the upcoming Christmas program. A healthy, vibrant church cannot function in a manner where it maximizes the differences and minimizes cooperation. United we stand and divided we will fall—or at least lose our credibility in the community.

The apostle Paul knew about such divisiveness. Just read his letters and you will discover Paul's major concern for unity in the body of Christ. One aspect of this biblical unity is found in the church's desire to work with their pastor.

WHAT GOD EXPECTS

As noted in chapter 4, your pastor is called in Ephesians 4:11–13 to equip and enable the rest of the church to do the work of the ministry. This call from God is to bring to maturity believers in Christ: "Speaking the truth in love, we will in all things grow up into him who is the Head, that is, Christ. From him the whole body, joined and held together by every supporting ligament, grows and builds itself up in love, as each part does its work" (4:15–16).

That last phrase is the key, "As each part does its work." Each person in the church has his own part given to him by the Lord to be done for the benefit of the whole church. The pastor is only one person and has only one part in the total work of the church. His work specifically is "to prepare God's people for works of service." He is to equip through teaching, training, and personal example. He is to enable them through encouragement, correction, and mutual support. The pastor has a significant part in the work of the church, but every other member has an equally significant part in his own way. Remember, as in the orchestra, if one instrument/person is missing or out of sync, the whole composition/church suffers.

In 1 Corinthians 12 Paul used a different metaphor for the pain of disunity. He described the church as the body of Christ. Just as a physical body has many members and each one does its part, so the body of Christ has many members, each one with its own function and service to perform. Every member of our physical body is vital to its proper functioning and good health. Every member of the spiritual body of Christ, the church, is vital to its proper functioning and good spiritual health. The pastor is one of the members, but only one. He has his special function and responsibility, but he is not to do all the work; he can't. When he tries, the body will malfunction; pain results. Just as the heart can't do the work of the arms, or the legs the work of the torso, or the hands the work of the stomach, so your pastor can't do the work of some other member of the church. Each member of the church is necessary to the church.

The Lord has given gifts to each believer to help do the work of the church. Your gift is designed to help other members and assist your pastor in the work of ministry. We will look at these gifts shortly. No one has all the gifts, but everyone has at least one. Two apostles, Paul and Peter, mentioned other gifts that we can identify with more readily.

+ *Just as each of us has one body with many members, and these members do not all have the same function, so in Christ we who are many form one body, and each member belongs to all the others. We have different gifts, according to the grace given us. If a man's gift is prophesying, let him use it in proportion to his faith. If it is serving, let him serve; if it is teaching, let him teach; if it is encouraging, let him encourage; if it is contributing to the needs of others, let him give generously; if it is leadership, let him govern diligently; if it is showing mercy, let him do it cheerfully.* (Romans 12:4–8)

Peter mentioned spiritual gifts:

+ *Offer hospitality to one another without grumbling. Each one should use whatever gift he has received to serve others, faithfully administering God's grace in its various forms. If anyone speaks, he should do it as one speaking the very words of God. If anyone serves, he should do it with the strength God provides, so that in all things God may be praised through Jesus Christ. To him be the glory and the power for ever and ever. Amen.* (1 Peter 4:9–11)

It is not necessary to go into much detail here on the ministry of the body and the exercise of spiritual gifts. But we should recognize the basic purposes of our gifts in order to properly understand the role of the pastor in the church. As we've seen, the church is a body with many members, the pastor being one of those members. He has his proper function, responsibility, and service within the church just as every member does. He is to serve faithfully and to use his gifts to the fullest in the service of Christ through his church. But he is not to do all the work of the church, nor even most of the work. He is to equip and to enable the rest of the members to do the work that is specifically theirs. He is to help them discover and exercise their gifts and to fulfill the work which God has given them.

YOUR PASTOR'S GIFT

According to the Scriptures, every pastor has gifts the Lord has given him.

- Some pastors have special gifting in teaching.
- Some pastors have special gifting in evangelism.
- Some pastors have special gifting in counseling or administration.
- Some pastors have special gifting in other areas of service in the church.

They are to exercise their gifts to the fullest and to use them in the service of our Lord and of His church, spending their time in their area of giftedness and doing the very best work they can in that area of service. C. Peter Wagner emphasizes this in his book on spiritual gifts: "The smoothest structure for growth is one which fully recognizes the leadership position of the pastor and frees him to utilize his spiritual gift or gifts."[1] That is where you as laity can help your pastor, as we will soon see.

WHAT MAN EXPECTS

But what is it that usually happens? Too many times the pastor, especially in smaller churches, is expected to be the one who gives the sermons, teaches an adult Sunday school class, teaches evening and midweek services, does the administration, the bookkeeping, is the counselor, visitation and evangelism leader, is the one to handle emergencies, provides comfort for the struggling (i.e., gets calls at all times of the day and night), and maybe even is the janitor and/or handyman/gardener if no one else covers these duties. He is the one who must give up his time with his family to meet needs, any needs. "After all, isn't he our pastor?"

But the local church that operates in this fashion is the loser. Its members have a pastor who does everything, but has less time to do the best. As we will see shortly, this was the problem the early church faced and addressed in Acts 6.

SEVEN QUALITIES OF A DYNAMIC BODY

A molding of the skills and abilities of the pastor and the church leadership is absolutely vital to the well-being of the church. Further, it is vital to the beginning of a dynamic team. A dynamic team is aware of its individual strengths and weaknesses and is confident in working together. A dynamic team is one where each member relies on others for assistance, feedback, and motivation. The pastor and the church, especially the leadership, must become a dynamic team.

We have identified seven qualities of this kind of team. As laity who are active in supporting your pastor, you need to understand these qualities to help your team—the local church—to become a dynamic body.

1. They Clearly State Their Mission and Goals.

Shared goals and a sense of direction will always lead to commitment. Most churches understand what needs to be done at any given moment but fail to maintain an overall focus. As the pastor teams up with the church, everyone must be involved in defining where they are going and why. This often should lead us to a motto that reflects the mission of the church and focuses the members in ministry.

For example, one large church in southern California defined its mission as "Touching Our Community with the Reality of Jesus Christ." That mission is broad enough to reflect diversity but clear enough to establish goals. Each year they established a theme within the broad boundaries of its mission, as shown:

1993: "93 in 93"
1994: "Expecting More in 94"
1995: "Gaining Strength, Giving Hope"
1996: "Gearing Up for the Harvest"
1997: "Excitement is Building: Advancing the Kingdom"

Many churches and their leadership are a lot like archers who might shoot arrows at a wall and, once the arrow has struck, proceed to approach the wall and draw bull's-eyes around the arrow. A dynamic team establishes their targets in advance and then begins to arm and shoot. Success is then highly measurable.

2. They Will Support One Another.

God has given us in nature a beautiful illustration of perfect teamwork. When the geese fly south for the winter, the strongest are called upon to lead. They not only break the wind but also set the pace and establish direction. When the key leader becomes tired, it drops to the back to recuperate. But no matter who is in the lead, everyone else is honking encouragement. Dynamic teams function in the same way, sharing leadership roles, giving every member an opportunity to lead, and "honking" encouragement to each other. Every person on your leadership team is a "10"—perfectly suited in his role . . . somewhere. Individually, they have strengths that become proportionately stronger when working together and supporting each other.

3. They Clearly Communicate.

If the church is to become all God calls it to be and impact the community our Lord has entrusted to it, the leadership team must talk openly and honestly. Each member should solicit suggestions from other members, fully considering what the others say and then building on their ideas. Too many churches resemble this model:

Communication Model A

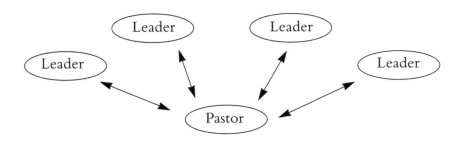

We are convinced this model functions poorly, because undo expectations and pressures rest solely upon the pastor. Communication Model B depicts a dynamic team in action, engaging team communication:

107

Communication Model B

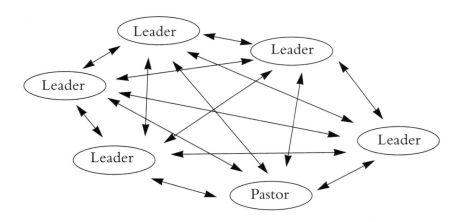

4. They Resolve Disagreements Quickly.

Any leadership team we ever work with will have disagreements. Not all disagreements are necessarily bad or destructive. However, a dynamic team identifies conflict, analyzes the causes, and defuses it expeditiously. Know that as laity you often can be used by God in a significant way to help quickly identify, define, and resolve disagreements.

5. They Build the Team on Individual Strengths.

Glen—the high school softball coach who once lost the team bus (chapter 3)—believes in constantly taking inventory of each player's skills and abilities. His ability as a coach would greatly diminish if he failed to allow players to play to their strengths. Likewise, leaders in the church must regularly catalog one another's knowledge, skills, and talents. A dynamic team is aware of their member's strengths and weaknesses, so they can effectively draw upon individual competencies. This is why we suggest that you as laity be well aware of your gifts and let your leaders know about your strengths and giftings.

6. They Make Objective Decisions.

Many things are never accomplished in the church, not because of lack of want, but because the "go-ahead" is never given. Dynamic teams have a well-established, proactive approach for both problem-solving and decision-making. Decisions are reached through consensus. In deciding by consensus, every team member should be able to "live with" and willingly support the decision or voluntarily step aside after expressing his or her feelings.

7. They Evaluate Their Own Effectiveness As a Team.

A team must routinely examine how well it is doing. A definite procedure should be in place not only to set goals (which is the first quality of a dynamic team) but also to evaluate whether the goals are being met and are appropriate. Proper evaluation can lead to modifying the goals, and setting new ones. We see the goal setting and revising process as a cycle, with four phases. This is shown below.

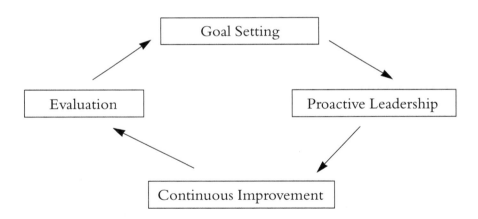

HOW ARE WE DOING AS A TEAM?

The following "Dynamic Team Assessment" will help lay leaders evaluate the team's effectiveness. If you are not in a leadership position, you may want to pass this assessment tool on to a leader. In rating your team, the leadership and pastor or pastoral staff should use the seven-point scale shown on the next page.

HEARTBEATS

DYNAMIC TEAM ASSESSMENT

For each characteristic of a dynamic team, rate your team on a scale of 1 to 7; circling a 7 means the team is exceptional, 4 means average, and a 1 means it is wholly deficient.

1. Clearly states their mission and goals

   1   2   3   4   5   6   7

2. Supports one another

   1   2   3   4   5   6   7

3. Clearly communicates

   1   2   3   4   5   6   7

4. Resolves disagreements quickly

   1   2   3   4   5   6   7

5. Builds on individual strengths

   1   2   3   4   5   6   7

6. Makes objective decisions

   1   2   3   4   5   6   7

7. Evaluates its own effectiveness

   1   2   3   4   5   6   7

TOTAL SCORE _____

Interpreting Your Score

> **45–49:** Congratulations! You are functioning as a team and you should seek to maintain this optimum performance.
>
> **37–44:** Not bad! You are doing fairly well as a team but realize that there is room for improvement.
>
> **30–36:** The team is having problems. Some of these problems may be minor; others may be serious. Nonetheless, your team must focus on the low scoring characteristic in order to rectify the situation.
>
> **29 or lower:** This is not a call to start over, but to seriously begin the process of working on the basics of team-building and recruiting other members who can aid in the building process.

As you have evaluated your team, you may see areas that need improvement. Ask yourself what you and other laity can do to improve the team.

FOUR PHASES OF EFFECTIVE MINISTRY

In the life of every growing and high-impact church, you will find common elements that can be identified. We believe there are four phases: drive, strive, thrive, and arrive. As we examine these four phases, we will discuss the characteristics and probable action steps vital in growing to the next phase of development.

Phase One: Drive

The pastor and members of the congregation have at least one thing in common. Both want the pastor to be the best pastor they have ever had. Whatever the differences might be, this common goal can strengthen their relationship and give them common ground for service together in the church.

How can laymen help their pastor be the best possible pastor? Ask your pastor. Get to know your pastor and his heart. Catch his vision. Ask him how you can be part of implementing his vision. Allow the vision to consume you, to drive you as it already is driving him and the leadership.

Unfortunately, we have seen numerous churches whose membership pulls in every direction with no commonality, no sense of oneness, and no unity in the body of believers. The result: No progress! The church is being pulled apart, going in many competing directions. You have only two options: Pull together or pull apart.

Often the key to reversing this dilemma is simply getting the church harnessed together with a unified drive, having the same motivation, excitement, and vision.

Phase Two: Strive

Once you have established a healthy drive for a ministry, you are ready to settle into the long pull—striving for the goal. Paul tells us in Philippians 3:14 that we are to do this type of striving, to "press on toward the goal to win the prize for which God has called me heavenward in Christ Jesus." God wants us to keep pursuing the goals He sets before us, both on an individual basis and as a church. When the Lord has called the church to a specific goal, then the church as a whole needs to strive towards that goal. As part of this, we encourage you to pour all your energies into the vision, the ministry.

Make one of your goals to take off the pastor's "plate" some of those lesser things you or others can do. Look for opportunities to help. Get as many fellow members involved as possible who are qualified. Know not only your own spiritual gifts but if possible those of the others in the church, in order to know how to best challenge individuals to be part of fulfilling the vision and ministry opportunities of your church. Be careful to do this in a way that includes the leadership so that you are not acting like an independent agent. Instead, be part of the team, in submission to the chain of command; you can act as an extra pair of eyes, ears, hands, and feet for the leadership.

As church leaders and the pastor strive toward the goal, be certain to know where you are in your course. Just as you don't get into your car, get on the freeway, steer the car in one direction, and then go to sleep as it speeds ahead, so you cannot take for granted that the direction you are headed in at one point will always be the way you are to go. Minor course adjustments are always needed. This is part of the striving—constant evaluation and expecting of yourself and others the very best service possible for the Lord.

During this phase, a key element to keeping unity in striving is to encourage those who are working and striving with you towards the goals, both leaders and laity. Too often we think that when leadership does a good job, they are simply doing what they are paid to do and need no thanks or encouragement. But tell that to the mother who has young children and yet manages the home well. She appreciates thanks for the meal and the clean home as much as her husband does for the check he brings home faithfully each month.

Come alongside those running the course with you. Show appreciation, give encouragement. Be a "honker." As you do this, you will be strengthening the ministry and helping it be more successful. What a great way to be an encourager to your pastor as he sees you helping people help him in reaching the goal.

Phase Three: Thrive

Keep a positive, healthy atmosphere so the ministry can thrive. This means that no matter what comes to bring discouragement, you are committed to pressing on and to helping others do the same. This is biblical teamwork. As in the striving phase, you keep the momentum going, you encourage others who may be falling behind, you come alongside those who need their hands lifted up or need a word of encouragement or even a hug. Above all, you keep praying for the ministry and all those involved to thrive, to be healthy, to stay on course.

Phase Four: Arrive

Congratulations! You have arrived at your goal. As a church it is wise to go back now and determine whether everything has been accomplished as you desired. Evaluate whether any new factors have caused a need for adjustment. Then finally, as success comes, determine if there is anything else not yet in place that should be done to maintain the desired ministry goals. But don't be satisfied with having arrived. Some people will accomplish a goal and then drop out because of the time, energy, and struggle it took to reach the goal. They want to kick back and let others do the work. They buy into the lie that they have done their share; now let others carry the ball. But our race is not to certain markers along the way. The race covers the whole of our life and will not be over until Christ returns. Therefore, if we are to win our race, we must be in the race for the long haul. We must allow the Lord to take us on to the next goal He has for us—and then to the next one and the next—until we reach the finish line.

As a lay person, you may not struggle with the desire to quit, but others do. So God can use you to encourage them to keep on keeping on. And in so doing you will be helping the church and assisting the pastor with people in a way he may not even be able to do himself, given his position. Yes, your input as a peer may be more powerful to the discouraged heart than even that of the pastor.

But what happens if the church, the leadership, and the pastor fail to reach the top of the mountain on the first try? What happens if unexpected intrusions disrupt the plans and changes are not welcomed as anticipated? What if one or two leaders have had difficulty buying into the vision or you felt like you had arrived but the momentum is fading?

When this happens, the church will need to go back to basics—go over the vision, making certain everyone is on the same page. Realize that the leadership and staff will need to step back, regroup, and maybe consider reevaluating its *drive* phase once again so as to maintain the initial vision and mission. As a member of the congregation, you can give them important input in understanding how people are feeling and insight into how to correct problems. You are a key part of this team in reaching and maintaining the goal.

AFTER REACHING THE GOAL

Sometimes we get so excited, even relieved when we've arrived at our goals, that we fail to take the steps necessary to see that things continue to run smoothly. You can play an important part in helping your pastor and staff not overlook this step. Too often we let down when we reach our goal because we've been so intent on reaching it. A building program is a prime example. The time has been grueling; everyone is stressed out. Then all of a sudden you've reached your goal. Pressure is off and too often the pastor feels so burned out, so beat up by the process of reaching the goal, that he wants to quit. And he too often does!

Therefore, at the end of a project, especially a difficult one, do things to encourage your pastor, to let him know you are still on the team, ready to help whenever needed. Members can consider doing something special for him and his family, like sending them on a short weekend vacation or buying him something he's always wanted but could not afford (or justify). Ask the Lord to show you and others creative ways to do this. We would highly recommend the book *Support Your Local Pastor,* by Wes Roberts (NavPress), which is chock-full of some wonderful, down-to-earth ways of encouraging your pastor. Among its many practical suggestions are giving him books, a magazine subscription, a health club membership, jogging with him, doing something for his kids and/or wife, having the church cover certain college expenses for his children, and presenting a gift certificate to his favorite restaurant.

Phase Five: Revive

For a variety of reasons, the goals at times will not be met. When that happens, a fifth phase is necessary: *revive.* This means going back to basics again, seeing where the vision needs refreshing or refining in order to meet the current situation. Missing the goals does not mean failure. It means opportunity.

As part of the laity, you can help "spread the word" by talking to others about your vision for the project, about why you are excited. You may well want to talk to those in leadership to get fresh ideas of how to present the vision. God may also use you to encourage them in knowing there are those who are still solidly behind the project and that the Lord therefore will bring to pass what He has shown them to do. With God's help, you can truly be part of bringing new life to something that needs to be revived.

A COMMON GOAL

A mutual understanding of what makes a good pastor and what God expects of your pastor is vital if you desire your minister to be the best pastor you ever had. This chapter has given specific ideas of what you can do to help your pastor become the best pastor you ever had. The chart below highlights seven areas mentioned in this chapter and earlier ones:

HEARTBEATS

SEVEN WAYS TO STRENGTHEN YOUR PASTOR'S HEART

1. *Follow his example.* Expect him to set a godly example, while allowing him to be human, to fail, and even to sin. Encourage him to set the example of godliness and follow that example in your own life.

2. *Support him as he carries the burden of his ministry.* He needs your prayers, your financial support, and most of all your love.

3. *Support his family.* Expect him to have his marriage and his house in order according to the Scriptures, but allow his wife and children to be themselves, to be like other members of the church and community. Don't set unfair expectations for them.

4. *Learn from his teaching.* His basic work as your pastor is to continue in prayer and the ministry of the Word. He is to teach you in the Scriptures, to encourage you, to correct and to rebuke with all authority. Listen, learn, accept, and follow his teaching of the Word of God.

5. *Let him minister to you.* Let him know when you are sick or you need his help. Accept his counsel. Work with him in planning and

directing the work of the church and encourage him to mature as a minister of the gospel.

6. *Work with him in the ministry of the church.* Allow him to minister according to his gifts. Exercise your gifts and talents fully in the work of the ministry of the church. Take your place along with your pastor as a member of the body, doing the work given by the Lord so that the body, the church, will be healthy, growing, and active.

7. *Encourage him regularly.* Encouraging words will lift his spirits and show him that you care about him in more ways than just ministry.

———————

Teamwork is critical to the success of your church. You can be used by God in a significant way to create an atmosphere in which your pastor senses the strong support he needs in order to lead your church well.

As you work together in the church doing the work of the church, following scriptural teachings in these things, you and your pastor will grow spiritually, and he may well become the best pastor you ever had. We like the illustration we heard recently of how one pastor feels like he is trying to hold together a pyramid of marbles. Just picture that! How can he succeed? He can't. But picture a number of hands that come to help him hold these marbles in place. Not an easy thing to do, but possible if there is good teamwork.

Closely related to biblical teamwork is the need to follow the lead of your pastor. Chapter 9 shines a spotlight on this need and how you can be an important part of the team.

9

following the leader

National Hockey League goalie Jacques Plante had turned toward the locker room after a poor performance, his head down. The red light above the net had lit repeatedly, signaling each score; Plante's team had lost. After the game, he told a badgering reporter, "How would you like a job where, if you made a mistake, a big red light goes on and 18,000 people boo?"

Commentator George Barna, recalling the scene, wrote: "Pastors sometimes go through periods when they feel like they are in the same type of pressure cooker of responsibility and judgment. And while they may find some comfort that the pulpit does not have a flashing red light attached to signal a sloppy service or a poor sermon, they are aware of the same type of evaluation as the goalie experiences."[1]

Many churches in America have an ecclesiology, or church structure and philosophy, that presumes suspicion toward pastoral leadership. Those churches build in a check-and-balance system to insure the pastor doesn't try to move the church in a direction the people do not like. The fact that the congregation sees the pastor as the head of the church rather than one from among a plurality of leaders reinforces members' fears. This is perfect ground for Satan to plant discord and doubt, encouraging fear of the pastor and his motives, and in general setting up a power struggle God never condones. And as pastors, we must confess that most pastors have those same doubts and suspicions about laity assailing them.

"FOLLOWERSHIP"

Both groups—church members and pastors—must be careful to identify enemy attacks and learn how to successfully resist them. Often the church looks to the pastor to be someone he was never intended to be. He is not the church parallel to the president of the United States. He is to be a servant-leader as Jesus was. Thus the church in America must regain a picture of both servanthood and "followership."

Right now you might be asking, "I know about servanthood, but what is followership?" Followership is a blend of godly attributes in a person's life that allows the kingdom to advance, pastors to be strengthened, and our own personal growth to be enhanced as Christlikeness develops. It also lets the world see the power of Christian unity as described in John 17 and played out in Acts.

What are these attributes of a godly follower? We want to suggest to you eight attributes that will allow you to glorify God as you follow your pastor's lead.

EIGHT QUALITIES OF A GODLY FOLLOWER

Craig Bryan Larson wrote in *Leadership,* "If a pastor isn't respected, the usual alternative is being humored or indulged."[2] Moving beyond indulging or humoring a pastor is more a matter of followership than flattery. We hope that these eight attributes help you move to being both a follower of Christ and His appointed leader in the church. You will notice that the first letter of each quality forms the acrostic "FOLLOWER."

1. Faith

The first ingredient is *faith.* Hebrews 11:1 defines faith as being ". . . sure of what we hope for and certain of what we do not see." Faith has nothing to do with your IQ; it has nothing to do with your giftedness. Faith is based on your trust in God, and in this case, the one whom He has given to your church to be your shepherd and leader. It is hard to follow someone you do not trust. Too often as laity, we find ourselves trying to evaluate things with our own understanding, from our own fleshly perspective. But when it comes to spiritual things, we need to have God's vision, and He says that is faith. In fact, He says that without faith it is impossible to please Him.

How does this apply to the church and your pastor? When you know that God has led you to call your pastor to shepherd you, and he responds to God's call through you, then you have entered into a trust/faith relationship with God. You trust the Lord to work through your pastor to accomplish all His purposes for the church. This does not mean the pastor is perfect, for he is not. But surprise! Neither are you. That is why we need the leading of the Lord. Your faith in Him and your trust in the one He has placed over you will allow the congregation to interact with him in finding God's will, and then following his lead in carrying it out.

When there are conflicts, faith helps you to work on resolving them in a fair way rather than imposing your will on the pastor and the church in general. Prayer puts oil on any troubled waters; it should be present in a significant way in all church planning. But prayer should also be an important ingredient of how any church member addresses differences of opinion between himself and the pastor. Pray for the Lord to show both of you what is truth. If you think your pastor is wrong, give him the benefit of the doubt. Realize that he sincerely believes he is right and therefore only needs for you to pray to the Lord to address the problem.

Now this takes a real exercise of faith considering the twenty-first century mind-set. It means that in a given area you may need to find Scripture to pray into the situation, and choose to keep silent, as James 3 suggests. It means having faith in God's great ability to be in control, to change hearts (Proverbs 21:1), or whatever else applies to a specific situation (Romans 8:28). Such faith will allow you to choose to pray that *God* shows your pastor the truth rather than for you to have to confront him.

As pastors we say this because by now you should have a sense of the amount of negative comments a pastor gets from all sides. That is why we strongly suggest that whenever possible you walk by faith in God and *His control,* rather than by sight and *your control.* Put God to the test. He says the righteous will live by faith. (See Habakkuk 2:4; Romans 1:17.) When you live by faith it is easy to follow your pastor's lead.

2. Others Focused

The second attribute of a godly follower is being *others focused.* Jesus came not only to set a model for your pastor, but for you, too. He said He came not "to be served, but to serve, and to give His life" (Mark 10:45). Being others focused is being willing to see a need *and* take personal responsibility to meet that need. The RQ list in chapter 2 provides a good starting point. It suggests a number of areas in which you and others can help the pastor help others by being an extension of his ministry in an area God has gifted you.

For example, he is expected to visit the elderly and the sick. Volunteer to do that for him. He may have to go once a month, but not twice if you take one of those visits. Can you counsel? If so, offer your services to counsel the less drastic needs of people. If appropriate, learn from him as a mentor how to counsel others. Maybe you could take all of the premarital counseling off his hands.

Ask God to show you how to focus on others. Soon you will be surprised at how you will see many opportunities and will begin seeing and feeling towards people as God sees and feels.

3. Loyalty

The first "L" in becoming a godly follower is *loyalty.* Often because of a church or individual's negative experience where loyalty became blind and discernment was lacking, a person has become predisposed to a life of suspicion rather than trust. A basic ingredient of loyalty is trust. Many leaders in the church today see their primary role as that of a watchdog, listening to the plans of the pastor and casting judgment on them. As a result, decisions become political as leaders think in terms of "How will the congregation respond to this?"

Remember, loyalty can transcend disagreement. Where faithfulness refers to a person's actions, loyalty is a picture of the person's heart.

HEARTBEATS

ATTRIBUTES OF A GODLY FOLLOWER

We believe there are eight attributes of a godly follower. To help you remember the qualities, we have arranged them in an acrostic that spells *FOLLOWER*. Develop these eight qualities in your life, and you will honor your pastor and serve all men and women effectively.

F *Faith.* Believe that God has led your church to call your pastor to shepherd you; trust that the Lord will work through your pastor to accomplish His purposes for the church.

O *Others focused.* Desire to serve (as Jesus did); look for a need and take responsibility to meet that need.

L *Loyalty.* Desire that your pastor succeed; you may disagree, but support his authority.

L *Leadership potential.* Develop your own leadership potential, recognizing that followers are learners (as leaders are) who have leadership potential.

O *Opportunist.* Make the most of every opportunity; be positive, looking for opportunities to help the pastor and others.

W *Worldwide vision.* See the possibilities by having a vision for your church and the world around you; look beyond problems to see possibilities.

E *Ethical.* Display integrity in all you do; show consistency in your words and actions.

R *Responsiveness.* Follow through in all you do so others can know you are dependable; complete all tasks.

Loyalty means that you want the one you serve to be successful. Both of us, Pastor Glenn and Pastor Glen, have people in our lives who are totally committed to the success of our ministry and kingdom impact. Those individuals whom we consider to be loyal friends and coworkers do not blindly follow us, yet they can be trusted in spite of disagreement. Therefore, true loyalty will not mean lack of disagreement; it simply mandates that when a problem arises it is the problem that is attacked and not the person. Loyalty provides protection so that when a problem arises, it is not allowed to affect the person's relationship with their pastor.

4. Leadership Potential

As the twenty-first century arrives, ministry demands flexibility and a hunger for growth and personal development. Leaders are learners. But let's go a step further: Followers also are learners and need to continue to develop their leadership potential in three areas.

Potential leaders first realize their indebtedness to God and the people whom God has placed in their lives. Some people come to church and wonder if God loves them and the church has a wonderful plan for their lives. But remember, there are no coincidences in the will of God—only God-incidences. Every trial, every valley, every mountaintop experience are all a part of God's active, molding hands on our lives. Many years ago Edith Schaeffer wrote *The Tapestry,* describing how our lives are simply a series of various colored threads, experiences that are interwoven into the fabric of our lives. God is weaving this wonderful tapestry. As we look back we can see He has moved in various events and through people.

Second, with leadership potential you choose to verbalize your appreciation and build people up on a daily basis. This includes doing such things as thanking people that have impacted your life or sending a note of encouragement for someone who has impacted your ministry or has been a mentor to you.

Third, leadership potential will visualize a more preferable future and do everything possible to support moving in that direction.

5. Opportunist

Usually we view an opportunist as being a scoundrel, a greedy manipulator, or a person without scruples. But actually, true opportunists are those who make the most of every opportunity. They tend to be positive people. Paul endorsed being an opportunist when he said in Ephesians 5:16 that we are to make "the most of every opportunity, because the days are evil." We are to "seize the day," and Ephesians 5:16 is the *carpe diem* of the Christian life.

Evangelism is a good place to see the opportunist in action. Opportunists will look for ways to share their faith. They will ask the Lord to open up conversations throughout their day to share with people, and they will look for creative ways to do just that. The opportunist will even take classes or study materials on the subject. He takes seriously the Lord's injunction in Ephesians we have just looked at.

The ones who are opportunists and want to come alongside the pastor may look at the RQ list in chapter 2, ask the Lord which one(s) they can help out with, and create their own opportunity to serve without having others initiate the request.

As pastors, we both have opportunists serving in our churches in the area of small groups. These opportunists have seen a need that was not filled, such as a group for single parents or a recovery group, and came to leadership with their ideas. Eventually those suggestions brought about a new group, often headed up by the opportunist. It has been our experience that often God will show a person the need for something that He wants that person to meet. The opportunist is a prime candidate for filling such needs.

6. Worldwide Vision

Followers with worldwide vision can see the big picture and support it. This person has a heart that is willing to expand to personalize the vision of the leadership.

During World War II, a worker in an East Coast factory was responsible for folding parachutes. Day in and day out, with almost a laborious repetitiveness, he folded parachutes for people who were going to be jumping into enemy lines in defense of freedom. When approached one day by a military correspondent and asked, "What keeps you motivated?" his answer was, "I always remember that I might be folding the parachute for the ones I love." This man, who had what appeared to be a mundane responsibility, had personalized it to include a much bigger picture.

A worldwide visionary sees possibilities. If something isn't working, he or she will refine or remove it in order to see the vision accomplished. Peter Drucker, one of the great business minds of our era, once said, "When the horse dies, dismount." God wants people to see beyond the problems to the possibilities. A worldwide vision empowers that.

Clearly Joshua and Caleb were visionaries. Part of a dozen spies who entered the Promised Land to size up the area, those two alone returned to say "Go." Have you discovered that the majority is not always right? A person with a worldwide vision sees beyond the giant problems and sees giant possibilities. That's one important reason that the Lord wants us to focus on Him and not on our problems. He has the big picture. He knows how to solve any problem, which to Him is no problem.

Our God has a worldwide vision. When we look at Him we can see with His eyes the bigger picture, and in so doing, our expanded vision will encourage our hearts to be successful followers.

7. Ethical

A follower displays the word *integrity* in his actions. Joe Stowell, president of Moody Bible Institute, wrote, "When ministries fail, it is most often not because we have failed to understand or even apply the best techniques and programmatic advances with the flock. We most often fail because we have either forgotten or have not known that the key to every ministry is the quality of the shepherd who leads."[3]

Stowell is absolutely right. The tragedy, however, is that we fail to apply to ourselves the standards we often have for others. Not only should there be integrity in the life of a leader but the same attributes should permeate the life of the follower. This means in all areas of life, not just at church or in the home.

At the workplace, a person needs to operate ethically. For many believers this can be a real challenge because the nature of their job lends itself to, and may seem to require, unethical practices. Sales is one area that comes to mind. What is your picture of the ethics of the used car salesman? Why? Does it have to be that way? The one who belongs to the Lord must live a godly life (1 Timothy 4:7–8). That is God's standard. So the used car salesman who is a believer needs to be honest in all he does. He needs to trust the Lord for His blessings even if in applying ethical standards he may lose a sale or get a lesser commission.

Ethics in business all too often boil down to, "How much do I trust the Lord?" We need to be convinced that when we put the Lord first in our lives, then He will take care of us in a much better way than we could ever do in an unethical way. And believe us, it is very difficult when you are counseling someone and explaining biblical principles that touch on a weak area in your own life. The conviction of your own words is so strong as to almost interfere in being able to verbalize what needs to be said. We have both experienced that "quick prayer" of confession to get us right with the Lord so we can say what we know He wants said.

The book of Proverbs is a wonderful source of helping to mold your ethics. We highly commend it to you for regular input.

8. Responsiveness

A genuine follower is one who will always come through—no excuses, no hesitation, and no regrets. They are responsive to the task and will do everything they can to follow through.

We are reminded of what happens when you baby a car, keeping it looking sharp on the outside, giving it regular washings and waxing and yet, when you turn on the key, it does not respond because you have not given it any fuel, an essential element if it is to respond. In the same way there are some essential ingredients in the life of a follower if he is to respond God's way:

- *Dependability.* Dependability is a must if a church is to operate well with its volunteers. There is nothing more frustrating to your pastor than to give something to a lay person and expect that it will be done well and on time, only to find out the person has dropped the ball and not responded in a responsible way.

- *Preparation.* Paul exhorted Timothy (and today's pastors) to "Preach the Word; be prepared in season and out of season" (2 Timothy 4:2). Similarly, the responsive follower will be ready for whatever task he or she has taken on. This means being prepared for Sunday school lessons, both as a teacher *and* as the student. It means having all your work ready when you come to a meeting and have a report. From a spiritual standpoint, it means you will be "prayed up," responding to the leading of the Spirit in whatever you do, and being a good follower of the Lord's direction not only in your daily life, but in whatever ministry assignments He entrusts you with.

- *Being a good finisher.* Paul wrote near the end of his life, "For I am already being poured out like a drink offering, and the time has come for my departure. . . . I have finished the race, I have kept the faith" (2 Timothy 4:6–7). In any church you will have those who start a job and then let it drop. This is frustrating to all who are affected. As a follower, you will want to finish well whatever task you are given. Believe us, your pastor will greatly appreciate knowing you are going to finish what you started.

- *Being able to bounce back* when problems arise. We have often challenged our congregations that we look for people in ministry to be marathon runners. Yet over the years we have discovered that perseverance is not a long race; it is a series of short races that follow one after another.

A responsive person is a lot like a running back who is handed the ball, responds to an opening in the line, and gains three or four yards, and hustles back to the huddle for the next play.

WHEN FOLLOWERS FOLLOW

What happens when leaders lead and followers follow? Look at Nehemiah, who caught a vision for the broken walls of his home city. God gave him a vision to rebuild, the people united under his leadership, and in fifty-two days the walls were up. Today you couldn't even get the permits in fifty-two days!

Next consider Joshua and Gideon. Joshua gained the vision of total conquest of the Promised Land. Five times God told him, "Be strong and very courageous." He accepted the challenge, the people followed, and not only did they enter the Promised Land, but the most fortified city on earth came tumbling down. Later, God put His hand upon Gideon and called him a "mighty man of valor." Was Gideon a mighty man? Not yet, but he accepted God's challenge to be a leader. When a handful of followers got behind the vision given to their leader, the Midianites were defeated.

Probably the finest example is that of the Lord Jesus Christ who molded an unlikely group into loyal, committed followers. Would you have selected His band of followers? A tax collector who had defrauded his countrymen? A couple of smelly, uneducated fishermen who would swing first and talk later? A "creative" accountant? Why would our Lord band this motley crew together? There is only one answer: He could use any loyal followers to advance the kingdom and accomplish the plan of salvation. During their three years with our Lord, the disciples whined, debated, and argued about who would be the greatest in the kingdom. After the resurrection they finally caught the vision. They changed from the curious to the convinced and finally to the committed.

It is through followers that Christ will turn the world upside down. It's through followers that the world will see that we are His disciples. And it will be as followers that we believe we will stand before God one day and hear, "Well done, thou good and faithful servant."

Having considered these eight attributes of a godly follower, take time to measure where you are on the road to followership. Complete the following survey, totaling your points. Then dedicate yourself toward becoming a great follower of your spiritual leaders, Jesus the Chief Shepherd and your pastor, the undershepherd of your church.

HEARTBEATS

HOW AM I DOING AS A FOLLOWER?

Measure your current level of followership by completing this survey. In measuring your degree of following the leader, rate your level on a scale of 1 to 7. Circling a 7 means your team is exceptional, *4* means average, and a *1* means it is wholly deficient.

Faith

| 1 | 2 | 3 | 4 | 5 | 6 | 7 |

Others Focused

| 1 | 2 | 3 | 4 | 5 | 6 | 7 |

Loyalty

| 1 | 2 | 3 | 4 | 5 | 6 | 7 |

Leadership Potential

| 1 | 2 | 3 | 4 | 5 | 6 | 7 |

Opportunist

| 1 | 2 | 3 | 4 | 5 | 6 | 7 |

Worldwide Vision

| 1 | 2 | 3 | 4 | 5 | 6 | 7 |

Ethical

| 1 | 2 | 3 | 4 | 5 | 6 | 7 |

Responsiveness

| 1 | 2 | 3 | 4 | 5 | 6 | 7 |

Total Score: _____

Interpreting Your Score:

43–56: You are well on your way to becoming a conscientious follower.

32–42: You are strong in some areas, but need to strengthen other specific areas.

22–31: Time to change!

1–21: What's a follower again?

10

seven qualities of an effective church

Teaching the Elephant to Dance is an excellent book on management and change. Author James Belasco begins with an account of the conditioning and training of circus elephants:

> Trainers shackle young elephants with heavy chains to deeply embedded stakes. In that way the elephant learns to stay in its place. Older elephants never try to leave even though they have the strength to pull the stake and move beyond. Their conditioning limits their movements with only a small metal bracelet around their foot—attached to nothing. . . . Yet when the circus tent catches on fire—and the elephant sees the flames with his own eyes and smells the smoke with its own nostrils—it forgets its old conditioning and changes. Your task: set a fire so your people see the flames with their own eyes and smell the smoke with their own nostrils—without burning the tent down.[1]

Our goal in this chapter is to set a fire in the heart of the reader, to allow you to smell the smoke of the lost condition of people all around you and motivate you to change, to become more effective in your ministry areas. By doing so, you will surely strengthen your pastor's heart. To help you in serving your church, we have identified seven qualities of an effective church. Such a church makes a difference for our Lord, as members break free from previous conditioning and move forward with a sense of urgency.

As we look at the following seven qualities of an effective church, we have divided each into three parts. For each of the seven qualities we will present the philosophy or reasoning behind the need for that quality, the pastor's role in providing this quality, and finally the laity's role. For both pastor and laity we offer suggestions to implement and/or maintain the quality.

A CLEAR-CUT, GOD-GIVEN VISION

The Scripture reminds us that "where there is no vision, the people perish" (Proverbs 29:18 KJV). Vision acts as an anchor to hold the church in place, as a strong mooring for the foundations of the church to rest upon. The first quality of an effective church is having a clear vision.

Sadly, too many churches today exist without a clear understanding of why they exist. They have no vision.

For our purposes here, we can use vision and mission interchangeably. As Loren Mead wrote in *The Once and Future Church,* "Where a sense of mission has been clear and compelling, the church has been sacrificial and heroic in its support of that mission."[2]

Here's how the pastor can promote this vision. The pastor:

- Enlists the lay leaders to help form the vision.
- Casts the vision.
- Keeps the vision before the people. Keeping the vision in front of the congregation lets everyone know where the church is in the process of reaching the vision.
- Evaluates periodically the church's progress toward fulfilling the vision.
- Determines and sees executed any necessary course corrections along the way.

How can the laity promote the vision? Each member can:

- Assist the pastor in clarifying the vision.

- Embrace the vision.
- Pray for the fulfillment of the vision.
- Seek God to identify his or her own part in reaching the vision.
- Help the church to reach the vision.
- Help new people to learn of the vision. This can be done through explaining how the church developed the vision and telling what you think of it. It can include expressing your excitement and telling how God is using you to help accomplish the vision. In preparing to talk with new people, ask God to show you how to communicate the vision and what ways to challenge the friend to embrace the vision and use their talents in accomplishing it.

A STRONG, WINNING TEAM

Second, an effective church builds and maintains a strong, winning team. For a team to win, it must create a winning climate. Part of this is choosing the right leaders to comprise the ministry team. The pastor can never, should never, be the whole "show" in a church. He needs to surround himself with a strong, winning team of staff and laity who are able to play a significant role in the running of the church.

Here's how the pastor can develop a strong team. The pastor can:

- Seek the Lord for whom He wants to fill each position. Prayer is essential.
- Select staff wisely, looking at the skills needed to help reach the goals and following the guidelines of your church's hiring policy. Most churches have staff needs that are beyond their current ability to fund. Therefore, the pastor needs to evaluate many elements, including the vision of the church, the ages and numbers of those attending, the availability of laity to take some of the workload, etc., in determining who should be hired, and even who should stay on staff if performance is not up to expectations. We also have seen the use of volunteer staff

as an effective alternative. Not everyone needs to be put on the church payroll to assume a ministry position of responsibility.

- Choose lay leaders who will make a significant contribution to the team. This means that the person may have administrative skills, discipling abilities, or other key skills or talents (often from his work experience) that will contribute to reaching the goals. Often such people can donate their time and save the church money in having to hire the services from outside. Such leaders need to be able to cooperate well with the team that is being built, should have a clear understanding of the vision and how it will be accomplished, and be reliable in completing assignments.

- Make certain there is a clear job description. Anyone who is doing a job, whether it is a paid position or a volunteer one, benefits from a clear spelling out of what is expected of him as well as what his responsibilities are. Duties and boundaries often need to be part of such a job description. Sometimes a description already exists. Where there is none, the pastor will need to create one or see that someone else does with his approval (or that of someone he designates). When a new position is being created, the pastor may well want to have the person being considered giving input. Included in the job description should be some method of reporting so supervision can be easier.

- Have periodic evaluations. As capable as a person may be, it is always wise to have and follow a reporting system. This should include a way for making suggestions and for sharing prayer requests and concerns. Such a system gives the pastor and/or his delegated authority the opportunity to discover problems before they get too big. It also is an excellent opportunity to express gratitude to the ones donating their time. For those on staff, it is an invaluable time of expressing continued support and giving encouragement where needed. It also keeps a person from feeling they are unnoticed and/or unappreciated.

- Provide opportunities for constructive input and/or criticism without senior ministry staff being threatened.

How can the laity help? Each member can:

- Cover in prayer the pastor and anyone else involved in the decision-making process.
- If so led by the Lord, let the pastor know he is available to help in any way. Offer suggestions, if appropriate, of ways you might help. But do not get offended if you are not considered for the project.
- Consider prayerfully any request from the pastor or others to fill a position. Do what the Lord shows even if it is not convenient.
- Be conscientious and do everything she can to complete all assignments she accepts with the highest standards.
- Pray regularly for the team.

THE INFLUENCERS

Third, those in an effective church know its influencers and enlist their support. The wise church leadership knows its people well enough to know who are the natural leaders and influencers in the congregation. The effective church will always be aware of both who they are and how they may respond to any given project, ministry, proposal, or change. The effective church leadership will recruit such influencers, educate them concerning the vision for the new idea, and then send them to help smooth the way for the acceptance of others.

Pity the poor leadership that has overlooked this key group of influencers and fails to bring them aboard before launching a project. Not to do so is to set yourself up for a high chance of failure. This one step, of informing the influencers and recruiting their support, can save a project and definitely cut down on potential troubles and pitfalls. It can help to neutralize the enemy attacks in a significant way.

Here's how the pastor can determine who are the influencers and recruit their support. The pastor can:

- Ask questions about positive people. Three key questions are: 1. Who will respond positively? 2. Who do they influence that may be reluctant or negative? 3. What is the best way to use their influence in a positive way to help insure the success of the project?

- Ask questions about negative people. Four key questions are: 1. Who is negative? 2. Why? (past history of not seeing this work, general attitude, critical spirit, hurt before by a similar project or something else, etc.) 3. Who does this person trust who could come alongside to help him come on board? 4. Does he need to be loved into position or given a stronger encouragement not to create the problem?

- Enlist prayers to redirect the focus of negative people. We suggest that the pastor seek a lot of prayer for any project that has the potential for someone to sabotage it. The prayer might run along these lines:

  Lord, You have led our church to do _____.
  [Be certain He has led you this way before praying this.]
  There are certain obstacles which seem to have the potential to block our accomplishing Your will. [Identify the obstacles.] Please intervene and keep any hindrances from occurring. Show us Your balance in how to address any problems that do arise. Show us how to pray for anyone who is still negative towards what You are leading us to do.
  May You get all the honor and glory as the project succeeds.

How can the laity help in motivating the "influencers" in the church? Each member can:

- Pray that the Lord will show the pastor those who have influence and how best to utilize them.

- If you are a person of influence—and most of us are to some degree in the circle of influence God has given us—from time to time ask, "How can I help You, Lord, in this project?" Often He will show you those He wants you to talk with. Depending upon your maturity, the situation, and the makeup of the leadership board, it will be advisable to consult them with what you sense you can contribute. This will help things to run more smoothly and avoid more than one person approaching the individual and running the risk of alienating him because he feels pressure from different sources.

PEOPLE-ORIENTED

A strong church does not have ministry just to have ministry. Instead, it looks at the needs of the people and develops ministry out of that. Jesus did this with the woman at the well. He addressed her need in order to evangelize her and the city of Samaria.

Here's how the pastor can keep those in the church friendly and focused on people. The pastor can:

- Guard against becoming a "lone ranger." He needs some protected time to himself, but in general he needs to be very involved with those who are on the front lines with others in ministry. He needs to do this either directly or as a person behind the scenes making certain things go well.

- Emphasize periodically the importance of being a people-oriented church.

- Model being people-oriented. This means being available when possible to talk, such as after the service or during office hours, or attending social functions for different church groups. However, depending on the size of the church, in larger churches it will not be wise for the senior pastor to be available to all of the congregation during the week.

- Consider developing small groups that meet the needs of the people. Their success can be one of the most significant keys to discipleship and keeping people enfolded. The pastor should have a part in helping determine which ones will be offered and who will be the leaders.

- Host a "Meet the Pastor" opportunity for all new members. This meeting would be at the pastor's home, although it could be held at the church if that were not practical. In this way the new people have a jump start on getting to know their pastor and learning his heart. It also makes them feel special and that he cares about people as individuals rather than as a "congregation" only.

As a member of the congregation, you can help in several ways:

• Try to greet new people, visitors. Avoid just talking to those you know, simply because you feel comfortable that way.

• Look for creative ways to show your care toward individuals. For example, some churches have one or more families assigned each Sunday to invite new people to their home for Sunday lunch. Others will be assigned to take out to lunch at a local restaurant anyone who comes as a visitor and has the time. (Even if they don't have the time, the invitation communicates caring.) You and your family may choose to invite new people to your home once a quarter to show hospitality and to share your experiences at the church.

ENCOURAGES POSITIVE ATTITUDES IN CONGREGATION

Fifth, a strong church exhibits positive, affirming attitudes. The apostle Paul wrote to the Philippians that his joy was complete when the believers there were "like-minded, having the same love, being one in spirit and purpose. Do nothing out of selfish ambition or vain conceit, but in humility consider others better than yourselves. Each of you should look not only to your own interests, but also to the interests of others" (2:2–4). We all are on the same team. Team members cheer for each other, encourage and support each other in what they are doing.

The opposite of encouragement is discouragement. Too often the church focuses on the "big sins" of stealing, killing, adultery, fornication, etc., and forgets how much God hates pride, gossip, and a tongue that damages others. Significantly, of the six things He hates as much as murder (Proverbs 6:16–17), three concern the tongue: "a lying tongue . . . a false witness who pours out lies and [one] who stirs up dissension" (vv. 17–19). As bad as adultery and fornication are, they do not make God's "big seven" list—lying tongues and rabble-rousers do.

Here's how the pastor can encourage positive attitudes among the people:

- Give a well-placed word of encouragement. Coming from the pastor, it almost always lifts the spirits. Staff and laity often blossom when they are encouraged by those they love and respect.
- Address criticism and gossip. When one ignores such words, they can become difficult to control later. The wise pastor will periodically address in his sermons ways to avoid and handle criticism. He will give the biblical principles for the control of the tongue and point out the devastation that can come with a critical spirit. A good pastor works with his staff to monitor the extent of criticism and gossip and responds accordingly.

How can the laity develop positive attitudes? Besides affirming each other in spoken and written word, church members can:

- Determine in their hearts before they ever hear criticism and gossip that they will not participate in ungodly communication. Usually laity will hear criticism and gossip before the staff does. Ask the Lord to show you how to neutralize any negative words you hear. This may mean: (1) questioning the source and/or accuracy of the information (where misunderstandings seem to be the source), or (2) pointing out your confidence and belief in the goodness and right motives of the person being criticized. At other times you may need to excuse yourself from the conversation as a way of not getting pulled into a negative conversation. If appropriate and you have the courage, say something like, "I do not want to be guilty of gossiping about this, so please let's not talk about this anymore."
- Pray positively for anyone who is stirring up problems with his tongue. James 3,4; Psalm 50:20; Proverbs 16:28; 20:3; 22:10; 26:17, 20–21; and Philippians 2:3 are good passages to turn into prayers. Pray these thoughts back to the Lord for yourself first, so that your words do not become a negative weapon against the person. With prayer, they can be turned into a posi-

tive instrument God can use to release His power into the situation.

A BALANCED MINISTRY

Sixth, a strong church has a balanced ministry. Too often church leaders can get burned out if they get out of biblical balance. Such balance has God as the top priority—a personal, growing relationship with Him. Next should come family; and then comes ministry. Take it from two experts in imbalance—we've learned the hard way that maintaining a right balance among all three is hard. Usually time pressures will cause our precious time with the Lord to get squeezed. When this happens, there is no possible way to keep the other two in balance.

The balance in the church is just as delicate. God designed the church to be in perfect balance, yet too often we go overboard in one direction. Too much evangelism, and fellowship suffers. Too much emphasis on fellowship, and everything else suffers. Too much emphasis on head knowledge from in-depth teaching to the exclusion of application can bring another subtle form of imbalance. We've seen some churches get out of balance with their Sunday school classes or small groups when they drift into an isolated state from the rest of the church.

The truly healthy, effective church also stays connected with the other parts of the body within its community. Isolation only produces negative results. What often looks healthy on the outside, in fact has the seeds of spiritual sickness internally. Such seeds can produce a critical spirit, judgmental attitude, pride, unforgiveness, and any of the other sins God hates when we separate ourselves from others who are part of His body.

Here are several ways the pastor can keep balance in his ministry:

- Maintain contact with a lost world. He should seek opportunities to touch his community. He should set an example of being a contagious Christian (John 17:15–17).

142

- Take evangelistic risks. Be creative and not afraid to try new things for the kingdom of God.

- Belong to a small group. People will be watching his personal commitment to balance.

- Get enough rest. *The effective pastor takes a day off!* Burnout is a reality we have addressed often in this book. When a pastor does not guard his personal time, he can easily get overloaded and still not accomplish everything. This opens him up to possible guilt feelings, which can push him even further off balance. We are convinced that burnout is a sharp weapon the enemy of our souls uses against pastors to first get them out of balance, and, in too many cases, eventually remove them from the ministry as they "burn out" for Jesus. But Jesus modeled the need for rest, so the pastor need not feel any condemnation for taking time to be away from the church, both in time alone and in relaxation with the family.

How can the laity assure a biblical balance in their lives, and therefore in their church? Church members can:

- Recognize they are a part of the Great Commission. We don't just pay the pastor to evangelize (Acts 1:8).

- Disciple someone. Be a part of the team that will raise up the next generation of godly people.

- Join a small group.

- Act upon the sermon. Make certain that what you learn on Sunday is something you practice all week long, all life long.

- Respect the pastor's day off. Don't call unless it is an emergency.

A TENACIOUS SPIRIT

Finally, a spirit of determination marks the effective church. Those with this kind of spirit hold onto their vision and their goals. They learn how to go through troubles triumphantly. They seek the Lord, not afraid to make corrections when needed, and bathe everything and everyone in much prayer. And above all, *they never give up.*

Problems are always part of any minister's life. The church that is accomplishing much for the Lord can expect to have great opposition from the enemy. That is why leaders need to be very wise and courageous. They must be willing to face head-on whatever battles occur. They cannot compromise. They will never give up; and yet they will be willing to make adjustments that are prudent when such adjustments do not compromise the vision, the direction the Lord has set them on.

As part of this tenacious spirit, they are willing to evaluate periodically how they are doing. The more honest and transparent they can be in their evaluation, the better the chance they have of reaching their goals God's way.

Here's how the pastor can develop and maintain a tenacious spirit:

- Set goals for the church without fear of potential doubters.
- Pray for the people constantly. He will make it his business to know what are the current important prayer needs of the staff and key laity. When possible, he will know of and pray for prayer requests turned into the office.
- Fill his own personal tanks. Remember, though, that while the pastor is "in Christ" and "in church," he can still be "in crisis." The tenacious pastor will read his Bible, get around encouraging people, and not forget his calling.
- Sense the Lord's high calling. A pastor needs to remember this in everything he does.

What can the laity do to maintain this spirit in the church? Each member can:

- Support the leadership goals. God has put this leadership in place for a reason.
- Pray for the pastor, leadership, and church ministry constantly.
- Remember that the pastor should not be his or her sole encourager.

• Maintain a kingdom perspective. Too many churches are filled with people who are more concerned with their turf than they are the advancement of God's kingdom. Paul could handle any obstacle because he had the right perspective, with his eyes fixed on the eternal (2 Corinthians 4:16–18). With that perspective, Paul could write, "We are hard pressed on every side, but not crushed; perplexed, but not in despair; persecuted, but not abandoned; struck down, but not destroyed" (2 Corinthians 4:8–9).

As you have gone through these seven areas, you may have noticed that for the laity, prayer plays a significant part. This does not mean a light "brushing" of prayer, but rather fervent "holding up in prayer of your pastor's hands." Do that, and you will strengthen your pastor's heart.

11

pastoral temptations

The apostle Paul describes the well-dressed Christian warrior in Ephesians 6:10–17. The belt of truth, the breastplate of righteousness and feet wearing the gospel of peace join with the shield of faith, the helmet of salvation, and the sword of the spirit to repel Satan's vigorous attack. With such armor the Christian can "stand against the devil's schemes. For our struggle," wrote the apostle Paul, "is not against flesh and blood, but against the rulers, against the authorities, against the powers of this dark world and against the spiritual forces of evil in the heavenly realms" (vv. 11–12).

However, because the Christian soldier is human, he is vulnerable to temptations. His sandals may well wear thin if they are not renewed (resoled) regularly. He can get a pebble in his shoe that will wear a hole in his foot, wounding him if it is not removed. Even the shield of faith may develop a hole as he constantly uses it to ward off "the flaming arrows" of the enemy (v. 16). If such holes are not repaired, he is vulnerable to being wounded by the enemy, taken out of the battle, or even killed.

Spiritual renewal is essential for you and your pastor. As we have noted, the Christian can be in Christ and still be in crisis. Our spiritual intimacy is crucial. Your pastor can have holes develop in his armor. With as much frontline battling as he does, it would be unusual if he did not have some areas that had holes. As part of knowing how to pray intelligently for your pastor, of understanding him better, we will be looking at some of the major areas that can develop weaknesses or holes in them. Then we will offer ways to help your pastor fortify his armor and strengthen his heart in God.

However, *one note of caution before you read this chapter. We share the following with you not to undermine your confidence in your pastor, but rather to help you understand more clearly who he is, what he faces in temptations, and how you can better pray for him. The statistics are simply statistics and in no way should be applied to any one pastor.* So please read this as general information, and do not try to draw a negative conclusion about your own pastor because of the prevalence of some of these weaknesses. Further, remember that some of the data and reports may sound discouraging, but God is greater than man's weaknesses. He will accomplish His good purposes through vulnerable men and women.

Also, know that even if your pastor may have a weakness in an area, that does not mean he has given in to it or is not dealing with it. Just as an angry temperament may or may not be displayed, so these weaknesses, with the control of the Holy Spirit, can be minimized, if not eliminated. The temptations may always be there, but one does not have to act on them.

OUR VULNERABLE PASTORS

Headlines concerning the moral failure of Christian leaders have revealed something every pastor has known—we all have our weaknesses. The average pastor is just that—average. Like all humans, he faces temptations. But most lay people expect him to rise above all those weaknesses, never have doubts, and be able to overcome whatever obstacles or temptations he encounters. Among their challenges are tensions in family life, attacks on his self-esteem, sexual temptation, and lack of close friends. As one 1991 survey of pastors showed:

- 90 percent of pastors worked more than 40 hours per week.
- 80 percent believed pastoral ministry negatively affected their family life.

- 33 percent said being in ministry was an outright hazard to their marriage.
- 75 percent reported a stress-related crisis at least once in ministry.
- 50 percent felt unable to meet the needs of the job.
- 90 percent felt inadequately trained to cope with ministry demands.
- 70 percent said they had lower self-esteem than when they started out.
- 40 percent reported a serious conflict with parishioners at least once a month.
- 37 percent had been involved in inappropriate sexual behavior with a church member.
- 70 percent said they had no close friend.[1]

Those findings give a very sobering picture of the ministry. To help you get a better picture of the pressures and temptations that can confront the pastor, we will look at seven different areas.

MORAL TEMPTATIONS

A wise man said, "Moral failure is never a blowout; it's always a slow leak." When people give their life to the Lord for full-time service, they almost always do it for the right reasons, including their love of the Lord and desire to see His kingdom furthered here on earth. We believe that no born-again pastor has ever gone into the pastorate to meet someone of the opposite sex or to "fool around." Yet a shocking 96 percent of pastors surveyed recently say they know a pastor who has committed a moral sin. This same survey found:

- 68 percent said the moral lapse had occurred with a member of the church.
- 66 percent admitted to sexual fantasies regarding people other than their spouses.
- 26 percent had a regular accountability relationship.
- 24 percent had sought counsel. [2]

Hear us well. Pastors are under huge attack from the enemy. Since the tendency towards moral failure is so inherit within the sin nature, pastors are candidates to be knocked out in whatever way the enemy can achieve—thus the growing pastoral exodus.

Lest you think this is an unreliable survey or just a fluke, consider these findings from a *Leadership* survey of three hundred pastors.

- 23 percent of pastors said they had acted inappropriately toward a person of the opposite sex.
- 12 percent confessed to having sexual intercourse outside marriage.
- 18 percent admitted to other forms of sexual misbehavior.[3]

Why are we seeing such a problem in moral standards? Well, look around. It is endemic in our society. Pastors have lived among the changes of the sexual revolution of the late twentieth century. Many have found their value system under attack and face a constant call to compromise their beliefs. In fact, this change in mores is one of five aspects of the ministry that has been identified by Louis McBurney as causing an increased vulnerability to infidelity. "People are encouraged to 'find themselves' through sexual encounters," McBurney has noted.[4] When absolutes have been removed or compromised in our society, even those committed to the right way can be tempted to compromise their moral standard.

Another reason for this moral weakness in the pastorate is the minister's duties as a counselor: Temptation can arise in counseling women or in having other close contacts with a woman on an ongoing basis. A successful pastor will be empathetic, feeling the pain of his flock, reaching out to them to help solve their problems. He has to be extremely careful not to let his emotions get too involved, or else he can find himself on a slip 'n slide to disaster.

Part of this problem is the human inclination to try to bond with someone who helps us through a crisis. Those receiving help through counseling are usually very grateful and sometimes can become dependent on the counselor's strength and wisdom. It often is just a short step from a woman's gratitude to an emotional attachment that desires physical expression. And the pastor may like feeling appreciated and needed, so he can become vulnerable to extended compliments. Meanwhile, the woman counselee probably has been denied love; as a result, she is looking for it and may misinterpret the kindness and understanding of her pastor as more than they are. A deadly combination, but one you can pray against and help release God's power into their lives to prevent any temptation from bearing fruit.

What You Can Do. It is evident sexual temptations confront a high percentage of our pastors. So what can you do about it as a lay person? The key way to aid our pastors is to cover them with prayer. Pray through a verse like Philippians 4:8, asking God to help the pastor think upon those things that are pure, or 2 Timothy 2:22, which tells Christians to flee from youthful lusts. As noted in an earlier survey, only one in four pastors (26 percent) had someone to whom they were accountable. So a church leader (or you) may recommend that he seek an accountability partner, who could let him voice his concerns and hold him accountable for his thoughts. Supporting him through accountability could greatly help cut down on giving in to temptation. Yes, the temptation may be there, but the Holy Spirit can use the face of the man/men he is accountable to and their questions on his recent sexual purity to put a damper on the pull of temptation. One *Leadership* survey found that 55 percent of pastors have no one with whom they can discuss sexual temptations.[5]

If you are a church leader, make sure the church setting does not lend itself to more temptation than is necessary. For example, is he expected to counsel the women of the church? If so, does he have a place to do this that does not require a closed door? If the door typically is closed, you may want to consider having a glass put in the door; or, as both of us do, have a secretary (or a volunteer in a smaller church) in the next room with the door ajar. (If you are not a leader, ask a deacon or elder about the counseling arrangement, and make the above recommendations, if necessary.) When Glen counsels a woman in her home, with or without her husband, he always brings his wife with him. Neither of us would counsel a woman alone.

As we have mentioned, pray regularly for the pastor to be able

151

to resist any and all temptations. Pray also that the women of the church will act appropriately and will be able to keep their emotions under control. Some pastors have found themselves the targets of women whose standards of morality are less than perfect.

MARITAL WEAKNESS

In most churches, pastors usually conduct the premarital counseling and counsel husbands and wives having marital difficulties. So you would think the senior ministers would know how to have the best marriages. Theoretically this is true; but in practice their own marriages often are one of the areas where pastors develop "holes." In fact, a recent survey in *Leadership* showed that one in three pastors (33 percent) are dissatisfied with the level of intimacy in their marriage, and one in four (24 percent) have received marital counseling.[6]

Four Areas of Marital Stress

In addition to the sexual temptations we have discussed, pastors face strong pressures in their marriages, which naturally come with being a pastor. Those pressures can lead to marital problems and even divorce.

Pastors H. B. London and Neil Wiseman have identified several significant stress points in a pastor's marriage; we will look at four.[7] The more you understand where such stresses originate, the better able you will be to support your pastor, to pray specifically for him, and, in some cases, to help diminish or even remove the sources of stress.

Competitive Vows

In the traditional vows taken at the altar between the pastor and his wife, no mention is made of his vocation as pastor. The vows speak only of his commitment to her. She well may have married him before he got the call to the pastorate, so she never saw God as her rival. But his ministry has vows too—he vows before the Lord to do everything God asks of him. A busy pastor may find that those vows keep him away from her more than either one would choose or like.

Further, the pastor's wife may not have the same level of commitment, nor may she have the same vision. Her focus is usually her family, especially the children. Both wife and children may feel shortchanged by their husband's/father's work, which regularly keeps him away from them in the best of times. Indeed, they may find their husband/father away for long hours when emergencies come or special projects such as a building campaign are in progress. Small children may not understand that Daddy can't be at their sporting event, dance recital, or other event because the Spencer family was in a terrible auto accident and Daddy had to minister to the Spencers one long Friday night at the hospital emergency room. The mother is left to answer the difficult questions, to wipe away the tears, and to try to help the children not resent the ministry that is competing for the attention of their daddy. She is having a hard enough time resisting the temptation for self-pity, and their woundedness just increases hers.

Incessant Emotional Overload on the Spouse

We've just looked at one kind of emotional drain on the pastor's wife. Other sources include church members not respecting her husband or playing politics at his expense. The constant pressure on him can spill over onto her, since very often the pastor's wife takes great offense at how others treat her beloved husband and what she sees it doing to him. She also has to try to keep his emotions on an even keel, but may give up after a period of time if he is constantly depressed or stressed out. Even if she does not give up, the unending pressure of worrying about his health and well-being can place enormous stress on her.

Women generally are more sensitive emotionally to situations than men are. Thus, the wife may feel greater offense at things than her husband feels. But because she does not want to add to his burden, she may suffer in silence. Eventually, she may explode, not necessarily because of what he has done (even though that may be a factor) but more from the tensions that have built up from her emotional overload.

Besides the pressures from his ministry, she may have to take an outside job just to make ends meet; or she may feel resentful watching other church members always buying while she and her family have to be careful, often feeling under the scrutiny of others for every penny they spend. When they do get the church to give more, it may have only been after some intensive, emotional words on both sides. At times she may feel like a beggar.

Out-of-Sync Schedules

Often a pastor's schedule will run from early morning with a 6 A.M. breakfast meeting until after 9 P.M., when the deacon meeting ends. By the time he arrives home, the children are in bed, and his exhausted wife is almost ready for bed. If she stays up to talk with him, they both are wiped out and he may have another long day tomorrow; so usually he chooses to get right to bed, without spending time with his spouse. Or maybe he still needs to work on his next message.

Thus any number of things can keep him from being with his wife, even though he is under the same roof. Also, there are constant phone interruptions at home. How much pastors grow to hate the sound of the telephone ringing!

Temptations Arising from Endless Contacts

The pastor sees many members of his congregation in many settings and roles during the week, not even counting Sunday. We have already noted that the pastor often has regular contacts with women through his counseling ministry. All these contacts together create much stress on the minister and his marriage. And if his wife, who might have less than a strong self-image, is not quite as pretty as his secretary, she may well allow suspicions to grow—whether founded or unfounded. Then one day she explodes—or implodes—from the fears and vain imaginings that have pressured her already overloaded emotional system.

What You Can Do. Your pastor's marriage needs to be bathed in prayer. *Power House,* Glen Martin's powerful book on praying for your church, contains an excellent section on pages 183–86 on how to pray for your pastor and his family. We would encourage you to use this as a resource for targeting strategic prayers for them.[8]

If you are on the ruling body of your church or in an accountability group for your pastor, and you see noticeable signs of trouble in his marriage, you may want to suggest to the others that they consider offering him free marital counseling (professional, from a retired pastor/missionary or a wise couple in your church or another church). As part of the accountability group, there should be questions on how the marriage is doing and anything the church can help with. In our last chapter we will be looking at other things you can do to support your pastor in his marriage.

Today you can find many wonderful marriage seminars designed to strengthen good marriages and help those in trouble. Consider sending your pastor and his wife to one. Also, there are organizations set up specifically to minister to pastors. A good friend of ours, Wes Roberts, has one.[9] He also has a service for referring people to other reputable organizations working with Christian leaders. He has weeded out those without a strong biblical emphasis, and only refers you to groups able to deal with your pastor without being "snowed" by a strong leader. (Too often pastors are so used to doing counseling that they are able to hide their true needs from the average counselor.)

You may also want to encourage the pastor to get an answering machine for his home phone if he does not have one. This way he can monitor his calls and only take those which are absolutely necessary to interrupt his time with his family. Just doing that will show his wife he cares and is trying to do something about the oppressiveness of the phone.

FINANCIAL WEAKNESS

Poverty in America has not gone away; many still live below the so-called "poverty line," a level of family income deemed just sufficient to meet the minimal needs of food, clothing, and shelter. Yet in one Arkansas church, only one family was below the poverty line. Sounds great, doesn't it? Paradoxically, the father had the skills to earn an adequate income. He was wise, a good communicator, and in fact supervised many others, all of whom live above the poverty line. Have you guessed by now that he is the pastor? As Paul would say, "Brethren, this ought not to be! A workman is worthy of his hire and should be paid according to his worth." (See 1 Timothy 5:17–18.)

Now, if your pastor is not worth paying a decent wage, then he shouldn't be your pastor in the first place. Of course, if each of the families in the congregation is tithing, but so poorly paid that they can't legitimately give any more, then this is a different issue. But it will be the rare church whose members do not have enough net income to properly support their pastor.

Nonetheless, our experiences over the years make us agree with one pastor who said, "It is almost as if the church members resent paying my salary, because it competes with things they would like to have for our church."[10] And, may we add, it competes with non-essential things that they would like to buy for themselves so they can keep up with the Joneses or simply fulfill their desires.

Both of us are consultants to churches. One of the things we often have to address to those who are in trouble is the salary they give their pastors. Too often the feeling of well-to-do members is that the pastor wants too large a salary—that he is being greedy. After we discuss his needs, many times we find he is not asking for more than is reasonable. And as we conclude our meetings, the members get into their fancy cars and drive off to their homes in the better parts of town. You can imagine how the pastor feels who is in such a situation. Yes, he may be wanting too much, but on the other hand he may not. You can obtain helpful data about appropriate pastoral and leader compensation by contacting the Christian Management Association and perhaps your denomination.[11]

Your pastor is probably is the equivalent of the chief executive officer (CEO) of your church. Should he have the extra pressure of an insufficient salary? We think not! Are we talking about scattered cases? No, for 70 percent of pastors interviewed in a 1992 *Leadership* survey said their financial compensation contributed to conflict and stress in their marriage.[12]

Most men receive a lot of their feelings of significance by being able to provide for the financial needs of their family. When the pastor is underpaid, his wife often has to go out and get a job. Significantly, one survey shows 69 percent of pastors' wives work outside the home (many out of financial necessity).[13] When his spouse works, the pastor may have to pick up the children from school or day care or take them to events because of her work schedule. There will be other responsibilities he may have to take on, including perhaps shopping. These extra responsibilities take away from his ministry, are an irritant to him, and deepen his feelings of inadequacy in needing to have his wife work.

Lest you think this is just the opinion of two pastors, let us quote from Christian counselor Louis McBurney: "Pastors frequently suffer from heavy financial stress. They find themselves caught in a Catch-22. They are underpaid and yet expected to live up to the lifestyle of their congregations. This bind is made worse by their attitudes about money."[14] We know pastors who rarely, if ever, have their church members pick up a restaurant bill. Yet those with whom they are meeting over a meal make a far greater salary than the pastor. If you want to see a great disparity, look at the difference in the vacation destinations of your pastor and those in the congregation.

As a church, you have the primary responsibility for supplying the financial needs of your pastor. He can be held hostage by your financial outlook. Sadly, we know of a few pastors for whom the desire for money has gotten out of balance. Not having money for a long time can do that to people.

What You Can Do. Pray for his finances, that your pastor would know how to manage them well and have sufficient supply for his needs. Proverbs 30:8 is a good verse to pray for your pastor and for yourself: "Give me neither poverty nor riches" (NASB). Ask the Lord to help your pastor keep his eyes on the Lord and not man and to "be content with what he has" (Philippians 4:11). But at the same time, be certain your church is being fair to him in being part of what God uses to meet his needs.

Look for warning signs: Does his family dress at the same level as most church members? Are they wearing the same clothes season after season with nothing new? How old is his car? How is it running? Do they attend functions that cost or is only the pastor represented? Does vacation time find them at home?

Church leaders can also educate the baby boomer segment about giving to God's work. Because of the "I-centeredness" of baby boomers, they often have little concept of tithing and give small amounts to God's work in the church. Baby boomers make up a large percentage of today's churches, so it is important to the financial health of the church for everyone, especially the boomers, to know God's standard on giving to the church. Both of us periodically sponsor an outside person who gives a seminar to the congregation on giving. There is always a noticeable improvement in giving after each seminar. If your church finances are limited, you might want to have such a seminar in conjunction with other churches and share the expenses.

We both have had the joy of having our respective churches send us and our families to visit missionary families on the field. This accomplishes two things. It gives the missionaries a boost they really need and seldom get as the pastor of a supporting church ministers to them, and it gives the pastor a way of adding for his family a special vacation (at the end) he could never afford otherwise. It is a triple win as the missionaries, pastoral family, and the church benefit from this investment.

When Glen went to Europe recently, he borrowed a camcorder from a church family and had his teenage son take videos of the missionaries as they were interviewed by Glen. The whole church family was thrilled to view their pastor in this on-site video, and the recent interviews gave church members a better understanding of the missionaries' lives and surroundings, and helped them pray more intelligently for them.

Many thoughtful churches will take up a love offering for their pastor at Christmas or Thanksgiving to show their affection for him and appreciation for him and his family. Such moneys are usually needed for important things—braces on teeth, a college education fund, or a better vacation for the family. We've rarely seen a pastor spend this money on fishing gear or something he wanted for himself. It almost always goes towards family needs.

CULTURAL TEMPTATIONS

Those living in the first half of the twentieth century accepted absolute standards based on Judeo-Christian values. This gave us a relatively healthy society, one which knew what was right and what was not. Whenever the wrong appeared, society recognized it and dealt with it. But things have changed. No longer does American or British society recognize that wrong is wrong and right is right. It has almost done a 180-degree turn and is now calling right wrong and wrong right. A recent George Barna survey revealed 68 percent say there are no cultural absolutes.[15] When there are no absolutes, life can get rocky, even scary. From 1960 to 1990, the U. S. population increased 41 percent, while violent crimes soared 560 percent; illegitimate births, 419 percent; and teen suicides, 200 percent.[16]

Many pastors are a product of this society and have had their value system impacted by it, at times finding it difficult to resist the lack of social restraints. This has affected both their messages and their vulnerability to temptations. First, their sermons sometimes reflect an openness to compromise, ignore, or rationalize the clear teachings of the Scriptures in order not to offend anyone. This has greatly affected sermons on matters of marriage and sexuality, including divorce, sexual behavior, cohabiting before marriage, out-of-wedlock children, and homosexuality.

Second, pastors have become more vulnerable to the temptations themselves. Pornography is a real problem for far too many pastors. Those of us who travel know how easy it is to watch X-rated movies in the privacy of our hotel room. No one sees but the Lord, and pastors can rationalize, "He will understand and forgive us."

Cultural temptations affect the pastor's flock too; they are being molded by a culture that worships success and power. This too often causes the congregation to hold their pastor in lower regard than congregations have in the past. Some members may even feel a sense of competition and engage in a power struggle with the pastor (and one another). This can bring out a negative side of any pastor or will contribute to depression and a lack of joy in ministry.

What You Can Do. How can you help your pastor resist cultural temptations? Pray, pray—and pray some more. You can never pray enough for your pastor, and in some areas of temptation, that may be your only way of helping. Pray for his purity according to verses such as Philippians 4:8: "Whatever is true, whatever is honorable, whatever is right, whatever is pure, whatever is lovely, whatever is of good repute, if there is any excellence and if anything worthy of praise, dwell on these things" (NASB). Add to that 1 John 3:3 which says, "And everyone who has this hope fixed on Him purifies himself, just as He is pure" (NASB), and you have a scriptural standard to pray into his life. Luke 12:48 indicates that those who have been given more, who have responsibilities, are held to a higher standard and have more expected of them. Ask the Lord to help your pastor recognize this truth and hold it as his standard for all areas of his life. Have an accountability group for him that will help him hold to a standard of purity. This group will often be composed of leadership.

EMOTIONAL WEAKNESS

In one day, Pastor Anderson's emotions went up and down like a yo-yo. From Friday night to Saturday morning he laughed and was inspired during Jim and Debbie's wedding rehearsal and the rehearsal dinner that followed. In bed at 11:15 P.M., Anderson awoke to a jarring telephone ring at 2:40 A.M. A female member of the church described how her husband had hit her and stormed out of the house. She sobbed loudly, and the pastor spent a half hour calming her; he then set up an appointment later in the day.

Saturday at 6 A.M. he arrived at the deacon's breakfast, where Deacon Jim said he was "noncommittal" about pastor's new ministry proposal. Jim, usually brusque, was powerful and persuasive. Many of the deacons liked pastor's new ministry idea, but few wanted to cross Jim. During the discussion, Pastor Anderson felt on edge and increasingly discouraged.

Later that morning he performed the funeral of Amy, a dear saint who died in her early fifties. She left behind four children—and one overworked husband. *What will they do?* friends and pastor wonder. The pastor offers words of comfort to the family and those present. Tears at times touch him as he, too, feels the sadness of the mourners even though Amy is now rejoicing in the presence of her Lord.

He barely has time to rush from the grave back to the church for a wedding. Mentally he tries to get himself out from the realm of sorrow and into celebrating the union of two beautiful lives. His emotions are like a yo-yo. He thinks, "Now, remind me again, why did I want to enter the ministry?!"

Such long hours and juxtaposition of opposing emotions in a short time is not uncommon in the pastorate. This pastor may well have gone on to counseling even others and/or had other meetings on this Saturday if his schedule had been too busy during the week. And the fact that he had to miss his son's baseball game did not add to his mental well-being. Guilt, even when you can't avoid the cause of it, takes its toll.

As we both travel around our nation, speaking at clergy conferences and teaching church growth seminars, we meet a growing number of pastors who confide they are discouraged and about ready to quit the pastorate. In order to reach that state, depression surely must have been present.

Seminary Professor Archibald Hart gives some insight into one cause of pastoral depression. "Post-adrenaline depression seems to be the most descriptive term I have found. A pastor should expect it on Monday after a demanding Sunday when he has had a long, continuous, heavy adrenaline drain."[17]

The pastor is always facing problems, even crises in the church and the lives of his people. His emotions are impacted. Frequently these emotions can produce tremendous mood swings in a short period of time as we saw in Pastor Anderson's going from the funeral to a wedding, to a tense counseling situation. If this happened only once a month, it might be less draining. But when it is a way of life and goes with the territory of pastoring, is it any wonder he may burn out?

Hart cites a Harvard Medical School study showing stress and burnout can lead to arrogance, addiction, aloneness, and adultery. Each negative starts in the mind, and Hart believes these four A's "are as much a risk for pastors as anyone in the secular world."[18]

This added stress can open another hole in his armor. The pastor, who is surrounded by much sexual temptation in the best of times, can fall into adultery when under stress, as he lets his guard down and allows an opportunistic woman to take advantage of his condition. He bears the blame, but stress was one of the weapons the enemy used to penetrate his armor and destroy his morality.

Your pastor entered into ministry usually because he loves people and feels God has gifted him to be able to make a contribution to their lives and to the kingdom. When his sheep start "biting" him through criticism, unkind or unthinking notes, and competition, these and so much more can leave your pastor discouraged, wounded, and depressed.

Want to get a snapshot of just how bad stress really is in the pastorate? A report in *Current Thoughts and Trends* newsletter indicates, "Long-term stress, according to the Alban Institute, is no stranger to American pastors. An estimated 20% of the nation's 300,000 clergy suffer from it. One recent year when the Southern Baptist Convention paid out $64 million in medical claims benefits for pastors' claims, stress-related illnesses were second in dollar amount only to maternity benefits."[19]

Emotional weakness can develop due to at least three other temptations, according to pastor and author Gordon MacDonald: (1) placing oneself above criticism, (2) developing a traveling lifestyle, and (3) becoming addicted to success.[20] First, the leader places himself above criticism. Pastors can display the weakness of needing to be in control at all times, of protecting their turf, and of being so self-confident that they do not allow anyone to challenge their decisions. This is actually a sign of weakness, for the person is insecure who will not let others question his decisions. Pride gets mixed in here, too.

Second, the pastor can develop "a traveling lifestyle." When a pastor gets into the public eye, as do many in the larger, more successful ministries, he will be called on to share with others his thoughts, how he succeeded and how to solve the problems of congregations. If he is not careful, pride can enter in, and he starts thinking of himself more highly than he ought (Romans 12:3).

Even if he is not the pastor of a large church, the minister still can become "addicted to success." In this scenario the pastor so loves success, he never attempts anything risky. Or he so wants to succeed he will do anything, even hurting people or running roughshod over them. Success becomes his god, his goal, the driving force in his life. God can and does get squeezed out in such a situation. Basically, success orientation is another form of self-love, of self-centeredness driven by the need to win, to be looked upon as a success. This psychological disorder will eventually cripple even the strongest of men and the best of ministries. God is a jealous God and will not allow us to replace Him with anything or anyone else, including ourselves.

What You Can Do. You can get away with running your car at 100 miles per hour for a short period, you can fail to change the oil for tens of thousands of miles, but at some point your punishing of the car will produce a breakdown. Your pastor is much like the car. He needs some relief from the pressures of ministry that psychologically impact him. You can help alleviate that pressure in several ways.

- As you understand his needs more, you can pray more intelligently for him. If he has an emotionally taxing schedule (like Pastor Anderson), ask the Lord to give him great discernment about those things he is dealing with. Pray for those who interact with him to respect him, and not to want their own ways, but only the Lord's ways.
- Make certain nothing you are doing adds to his mental stress.
- Encourage him whenever possible, both orally and in writing.

SPIRITUAL TEMPTATIONS

As noted in chapter 5, your pastor must keep himself spiritually healthy by feeding regularly on the Word (apart from message preparation) and spending significant time in prayer. If he does not regularly maintain his own spiritual health, he will be unable to minister effectively to his people.

One survey of 572 pastors found that a majority of pastors, 57 percent, spend less than twenty minutes a day in prayer; only 9 percent indicated that they spend over one hour daily.[21] Yet isn't prayer so key that the apostles in Acts 6:4 say it is one of the two things they must devote themselves to? In order to do this, they had to reassign to others many of the things that had crowded out their study of the Word and prayer.

As we enter the twenty-first century, pastors, like their congregations, are finding the good things of their ministries squeezing out the best and most important. As a result, the spiritual lives of our pastors is suffering, and so in turn are the congregations. Is it any wonder so many pastors are leaving their ministries? How can you minister on an empty tank and endure the pressures, the stresses that are a natural part of the pastorate?!

What You Can Do. Members of churches must structure time for the pastor to allow him adequate time with the Lord. Help those who determine the scope of his duties to see the absolute necessity of giving him, even insisting that he have, quality time daily with God. Those to whom he is accountable can play an important part in seeing he protects this time no matter what the pressures of ministry. Pray that he remains faithful in maintaining a healthy spiritual life, for you can be certain the enemy will be strongly targeting him in this area.

FEAR OF PEOPLE'S OPINIONS

One final temptation plagues virtually every pastor: the fear of what people say. Pastors constantly are concerned with how others respond to their sermons, to their ideas, to them as individuals. It can get so bad that some become almost paralyzed with fear and are unable to act according to what they know to be God's will in a situation. Sometimes pastors will not speak about certain subjects in their sermons lest they offend the rich or influential people who have this sin. Nor do they address the issues in private to the offending party. This temptation to heed people's preferences is widespread. It is easy to succumb to the fear of man.

To resist the fear of man is not always easy. We know of one pastor who lost his church because he did not seek to please the people. He took an unpopular stand, one that offended the "patriarch" of the church. The influential member's daughter taught high schoolers, and she told the teens she would never forgive a certain person for what had happened during a church split. The pastor tried to counsel her, but she stubbornly resisted any attempt to grant forgiveness. She openly defied the pastor and what the Scriptures taught. As a servant of the Lord, he was left with no choice but to ask that she step down from her position.

That was the beginning of the end of his ministry at that church. But the Lord used his faithfulness to Him to bless that pastor with a greater ministry and has given him influence he would never have gained had he stayed at that church. Thus, what the enemy of his soul meant for bad, God turned to good. Nevertheless, the sin still remained at that church and the end result was its dissolution.

What You Can Do. For most pastors, to stand against the influential is difficult. So as a lay person, you can pray for your pastor, that God will give him the courage to withstand whatever human pressures he may face. Ask that those who would be tempted to wield undo influence will back off, come under conviction, and start working with the pastor rather than against or in competition with him. Romans 12:18 is for everyone in the church. "If it is possible, as far as it depends on you, live at peace with everyone."

In addition, use whatever influence you have with others to encourage everyone to support the pastor and not to criticize. Interact with those who have to determine whether their opposition is rooted in biblical principles or personal desires. If neither the pastor nor the one coming against him is standing on a biblical principle, but rather is only trying to exercise his own opinion, then encourage the two to talk through their differences; or offer to have someone else mediate the problem, someone they both trust and who has discernment.

FINAL THOUGHTS

We've looked at some major areas of temptation for pastors and what you can do to help your pastor overcome or deal with each one. As you will notice, prayer is a very high priority in this process. You can never pray too much for your pastor, his wife, or his children. Saturate them with prayer. Let them know you are standing behind them in prayer and the Word. However, use great wisdom in telling them you are praying for a specific weakness unless he brings it up to you.

Ask your pastor periodically for prayer requests, so he knows this is not a temporary burst of prayer for him but is ongoing. Find out the answers to your prayers. We often tell someone we will pray for something, may do so at the time, and then forget about it. When you ask him how a specific problem turned out, he will be so encouraged and will truly know you cared, you prayed, and that the Lord is using you. The Lord can use you, therefore, even more to strengthen your pastor and to support him.

We are now ready to look more closely at various ways you can support your pastor, openly and behind the scenes.

12

how to support your pastor

We have a mutual friend, Dian, who has told each of us at different times, "I don't see how you can be a pastor. It is such a difficult, often thankless job. How do you ever bear the pressures, the infighting, the overload? Being a pastor is the last thing I would ever want to do." Now, Dian has been a missionary for twenty-nine years, served in Beirut, Lebanon, for eight years, with bullets and bombs flying around for six of those years. She never left to escape, but stayed in the thick of it. Could either of us do that? No thank you! But God called her to serve in this way, equipped her to be able to withstand the pressures of war, and she did so with much joy. She had a call and the blessing of God to be able to stick it out in Beirut and serve Him.

In the same way, God calls each pastor to serve in pastoral ministry. We and other pastors know that the God who called us has also designed the pastorate to be successful. He equips His servants to meet the difficulties, to withstand the pressures and the attacks, and to come through each battle stronger and able to meet the next battle with greater insight and strength. But as we have emphasized, God intends that the church members support the pastor and other ministerial staff. In a crucial way, God equips the pastor for success.

All good secretaries will tell you that one of the important elements of their job is to make their bosses look good. The boss is the one in the "limelight," but he never succeeds to the degree he is capable of if he does not have a competent secretary. Now, laity is not exactly the same to the pastor as a secretary is to her boss; but there are some striking similarities. Both should have the interest of the "organization" (i.e., church) at heart. They should want to see it succeed. When the leader succeeds, the whole is usually successful. So as laity you can help your pastor become the best leader he can possibly be. We have mentioned throughout this book a number of ways to give support, but here we will pull together many of those ideas and add some new ones.

To help you reach your goal of giving significant support, we have identified six areas in which meaningful support can and should be given to any pastor.

PERSONAL SUPPORT

Personal support occurs when another person comes alongside the minister to monitor and guide. Every great leader who is serving the Lord can never get away from the need to be held accountable. This is God's way, as we can see from several men in the Scriptures.

Accountability

David was a great servant of the Lord. But he had the prophet Nathan whom God sent to hold him accountable when David violated God's command.

David displayed a weakness men can have when they are at the top of the ladder of life. They can become so powerful that they believe they are above the law, even though they may be the one held responsible to enforce the law. David used his power to get what he wanted even though he knew what he desired was a sin. Thus, he forced his will on Bathsheba, caused his military men to set up the death of her husband, and then did nothing to correct any of his sins until Nathan came and held his feet to God's fire of accountability.

Sin often has a wider impact than just those committing it, and this case was no exception. The Israelites suffered for David's sins, for the kingdom was damaged by the punishment God gave. There is no record of anyone trying to stop David's evil plans. They all complied even though they may have understood what was going on and not approved. How much better if David had been a man who could have been approached and held accountable for his planned ungodly acts. What heartache and suffering he would have saved himself and his family; for we are told that the evil acts of his son, Absalom, were a direct fallout of his sin with Bathsheba.

Surely if anyone could be exempt from accountability, Paul should have qualified. He was well trained in the Scriptures (not to mention writing Scripture), an apostle. Who dares hold this man accountable! Yet, in the New Testament we see Paul in relationships where he holds others accountable, and they hold him accountable. There's Paul in relationship with Barnabas, with Silas, and with Timothy. We are certain this accountability was not in a narrow, stifling form. Instead, it was surely given in a way that helped Paul to accomplish his ministry.

Advising and Mentoring

Another form of help is given in an area we now call mentoring. Barnabas was a mentor to Paul. As a longtime believer and leader in the Christian community, Barnabas had the wisdom to help Paul through what otherwise might be difficult waters where he easily could make a mistake. Barnabas was able to help open doors for Paul, to smooth the way for Paul's acceptance by the Christian community. He taught him the ropes, suggested strategies, and in general befriended Paul to the extent that Paul, although younger than Barnabas, became the leader, with Barnabas taking the second position to Paul's lead.

Our churches have not outgrown this biblical model. Today pastors need help from the laity. Glen and Glenn both depend on the great wisdom and insights of our lay leaders and others to know how best to approach such things as building programs. In the current building program at Community Baptist Church in Manhattan Beach on California's Pacific Coast, I (Glen) have depended upon several key lay leaders. Their help has been invaluable in educating me in what would and would not be accepted by the whole, and who I needed to go to in order to help them catch the vision of the benefits of the building program, and how we could accomplish it in the best way.

My mentors have been invaluable as we've worked through each phase of this program from its inception, seeking the Lord's face, and in turn allowing Him to show us, often through the experience and wisdom of the laity, how best to proceed.

Glenn is near the Atlantic Coast, and he remembers his decision to become the senior pastor of Calvary Church in Charlotte, North Carolina. "The prayer, counsel, and even hard questions that laymen I hold in high esteem asked me were extremely valuable in discovering God's will."

Sometimes wisdom dictates that the mentor role come from outside the local church in order for the pastor to have the freedom to share his heart, his concerns, and receive godly counsel. As pastors, we have strong inclinations to keep our most difficult problems to ourselves, especially if there is a weakness involved. For anyone in our congregation to know could, if the person hearing the problem was not discrete or mature enough to handle the information without letting it affect his relationship with the pastor, turn into a disaster or at least the loss of the respect of the individual. Remember, we pastors are not superhuman. So the mentoring role may be filled from outside your membership.

Another source of mentoring can come, especially in a denominational church, from older pastors. They become like Barnabas to a young Paul. This gives stability to the younger pastor's life, to his family, and his church. How powerful it is to give older pastors a way of passing on the rich wisdom and wealth of experience they have so that younger pastors can avoid mistakes and grow more quickly. When appropriate, as laity you can encourage your pastor to link up with an older pastor in a mentoring relationship. Sometimes retired pastors, even ones in your own church, can serve in this strategic role.

DAILY SUPPORT

Doing something you love can sometimes be dangerous to your health. You get so caught up in the project that you can easily forget to eat right or get enough rest. Relationships can also suffer. Pastors love their work, or at least in theory they do. Just as in the business world, they can get caught in the trap of spending too much time doing hands-on ministry.

As we have already seen, the amount of things a pastor can do, if he has the time, and should do even if he does not, are many more than he actually can accomplish. He may well feel guilty about taking legitimate "downtime" unless he has the support of the laity, especially the leadership, in this. Indeed, many pastors will not ask for time off, thinking it is a sign of weakness. Others don't want to face the risk of being rejected. Whatever the reason, the request never comes. And what downtime is taken can be guilt producing, even though it truly is needed.

Encourage "Downtime"

Laity to the rescue! If you are a church leader, encourage the ruling body to give the pastor permission for downtime, a regular time off each week or month. Approach your pastor, suggest to him that he is only human, and, like all the rest of us, needs some downtime weekly if he is going to make it for the long haul. Tell him you love him and want the best for him. You don't want to see him burn out in ministry, and that is likely to happen if he keeps up the constant pace he has set for himself.

Giving your pastor this permission can be a wonderful gift. He knows he needs it but has simply not had the courage to ask. You not only will bless him by encouraging him, but you can be certain his ministry will reflect the benefits as he regains his strength and enthusiasm.

Downtime may be as little as a twenty-minute rest break each day, or a part of a day each week to a full day off once a month. Depending on the schedule and the size of the church, the downtime will vary; the pastor may need to be flexible. But he does need that time for physical renewal. Both of us, for example, like to spend a portion of our downtime at sporting events involving our children. We are grateful to churches that give us the flexibility, even if it comes between the hours of 8 A.M. and 5 P.M. during the week. Recognize the value of such times and encourage your pastor to regularly take them. Remember, his family is his ministry, too.

Your pastor is not a machine, and he has good reason to "come apart," as Jesus encouraged his disciples to do who were ministering at an intense pace with many pressures from their "congregations." Either your pastor will come apart for rest, or he will come apart.

Encourage Significant Study and Prayer Time

A. W. Tozer spent the first two hours of the morning praying along the lakeshore in Chicago. This was a restful setting and yet an important time of prayer. His enormous strength in the pulpit and in print came from this daily habit of prayer. The church enabled him to engage in prayer by giving him permission to have these first two hours alone. Support your pastor in this area. Let him know how important you feel it is for him to have quality, extended times with the Lord.

As pastors who are interested in how churches are managed around the world, we have noticed an intriguing difference between the church styles of our English cousins and our own American ways. The English pastors have "studies," while we have "offices." The word image speaks volumes to the way we tend to manage our churches as a business here in America versus emphasizing the time in studying God's Word. Add to that the fact that English pastors are regarded as teachers of the Word, while American pastors are usually seen as a CEO, and you catch the ministry versus business philosophy of the two. We need to encourage our pastor in his times of study.

This is not to say that there are not exceptions to this pattern. Glenn knows one pastor friend who has a wonderful library which the church helped him build. They recognized the need for him to be deeply in the Word and to have quick access to the tools that will help him be the teacher and pastor they need. This congregation encourages him to retreat every morning to his study. Surely this has contributed to his long and successful ministry.

Encourage in Writing

Pastors receive so many negative letters on a regular basis. Too often people who have a complaint feel they need to put it in writing to their pastor. Long after the writers have forgotten their wounding words, the pastor will still be able to quote the offending passages. Even the best pastors get them.

So why not counter such letters with a note or letter telling the pastor how much a specific message meant to you and/or a family member? Tell him how much you appreciate his long hours of service, the way he prays with people, or whatever it is that you've noticed that can be complimented. Make it sincere, and he will treasure it.

RECREATIONAL SUPPORT

Why does the world have the trite saying, "All work and no play makes Johnny a dull boy?" Because experts have observed the negative impact an excess of work can have on a person. The pastorate is not exempt from this truth. Your pastor needs his day off, just like he needs some downtime during his workday. This is not an idea that originated with pastors. It goes clear back to the time of Creation when God modeled for humanity that one day in every seven needs to be taken off.

We suggest that whoever is part of the accountability group you have for your pastor stay aware of whether he is actually taking a day off. Now this may be a day with his family and an exhausting one at that, but it is getting away from the pressures that is the important part. He will come home exhausted, but hopefully refreshed as his mind has had a relief from all the responsibilities that are constantly weighing on him. If he does not get his day off, then his energy level may well start waning, which can be another warning signal to look for, indicating he is not getting the rest he needs. So watch for those telltale signs—changes in mood, outlook, energy level, or appearance.

Create Opportunities

We both love sports. Yet it is hard to fit them into our schedules. But we each have some wise elders and lay leaders who love us so much they invite us to golf or play basketball with them. Now, we're not sure if they are just trying to give our poor out-of-shape bodies some exercise, or if they are looking for the companionship and an easy person to beat. Either way it is a win-win situation for us. Guess how much the trust level raises as pastors and laity spend recreational time together and see each other in a less formal setting? Then, if something just has to be talked about, such a relaxed setting often allows a less threatening form of discussion than happens in scheduled meetings.

Give Recreational Gifts

Both of us have loving members who surprise us every once in a while with great ways of taking some time off in a meaningful way. We've both gotten tickets to local professional sporting events, have had fishing trips offered, and time away at various condos owned by members. Many pastors have such a limited budget that these thoughtful gifts really mean something to them, in part because they can take their loved ones with them and treat them to something that would be hard to have otherwise.

Your church may want to consider giving a trip to a fancy hotel. Some travel agent friends have told us about inexpensive but fun getaway specials with breakfast included. What a great gift for your pastor.

FAMILY SUPPORT

Support the Pastor's Wife

Both of us have had the privilege of being part of the powerful work God is doing through Promise Keepers and its impact on marriages. We have often heard its founder, Bill McCartney, say a very sobering thing: "You can tell the success of a man in his marriage by his wife's face." When Bill first heard this statement, he looked into the face of his beloved wife, Lyndi, and what he saw let him know for the first time that he was a failure as a husband. Bill had time to reverse the damage in his marriage, and today his marriage is on solid ground.

Some pastors' wives have facial expressions similar to Lyndi's. Most pastors have supported their wives, but the women still have floundered. Why? Many pastors' wives feel frustration, even depression, from the words of church members who criticize their husband or children or expectations members have of pastors' wives (see pages 69–70, 85). As we've already seen, being a pastor's wife brings certain pressures. Women are sensitive and fiercely supportive of their husbands; a pastor's wife is no different. The criticisms he receives, the tensions at church, whatever power struggles are going on can often affect her more than they do him. Even if she is a quiet woman, she still has sensitivities and feelings, usually more than the more outspoken wife, and is vulnerable to hurt from the unthinking church members and their responses to her husband, her children, as well as herself.

The pastor's wife is just as isolated from being able to share her inner self with others as is her husband. She feels the pain he experiences from the biting of the flock. But to whom in the congregation does she complain that she is hurting or that her husband is neglecting her and the children? No one; nor will she tell anyone if he has grown cold in his lovemaking, or is just too tired and/or uptight to really spend quality time with the family. She loves this man. She wants to protect him, to have others think the best of him, even though he has clay feet the same as everyone else. So in an effort to protect his image, or perhaps in stewing over the negatives, she lets herself become hurt or even destroyed.

Friends, this ought not to be. We need to support the one God has brought to be our shepherd, which includes supporting his wife and children. This means words of affirmation and acceptance, not criticism. Paul tells us that we are to encourage one another, to build others up, not tear them down.

Give Encouragement

Be an encourager. It is such an easy yet important way of supporting your pastor and his wife. Ask the Lord to give you opportunities to say positive things about each member of the pastor's family. Make sure she knows these things. She needs to hear them. Unfortunately, sometimes we men have our heads in the clouds when it comes to passing on compliments.

Respect Their Time at Home

Any good marriage needs times of periodic renewal in order to stay healthy. Just because he is in ministry does not mean that this fact is any less true for your pastor. Indeed, the pressures of ministry make it almost mandatory that he be given support and help.

The amount of uninterrupted time your pastor and his wife have together is much less than it is for probably any other couple in your congregation. Pastors may be at home, but their phones still work. It never ceases to amaze us how consistently emergencies, crises, deaths, and other problems have an uncanny way of happening in the middle of the night, or when the pastor and his wife are doing something important—like talking, attending the kids' games, their school play, or simply enjoying each other's company.

Special Help During Stressful Times

Escapes can be especially helpful when your pastor is under particular stress. At such times, you and others can offer a change of setting. Over the years we have each received some special help from our laity. Wayne Detzler, who has pastored in England, told Glenn of one great gift—time away in a lush valley in Wales: "There was a time of sustained high stress in my life and ministry. A sensitive friend made it possible for my wife and me to go to the Wye Valley in Wales each week. What a refreshing time that was! How significant these times were in getting us through this trying period. I shudder to think where our marriage might be if God had not used my friend in this significant way."

There are several ways a church can minister to their minister, including some very meaningful escapes. I (Glenn) served in one church that yearly showed their loving support by giving Susan and me an all-expense-paid trip to a conference, adding an extra day or two just for us. To this day we remember those times with much pleasure. Each conference was so rejuvenating—to be able to change our setting, to be a couple just like everyone else, with no responsibilities, no messages that have to be polished, no concern that this refreshing time was about to come to a screeching halt with an emergency. And it was so great to see our dear friends at the conference. I always came back with recharged batteries and feeling even closer to Susan. And I could see that it was special for her, also. Such support from our church family was very appreciated.

Indeed, such a package truly supports the pastor and his wife as well as giving him valuable information and inspiration.

Other Ways to Support the Family

Gifts for Special Occasions. Wedding anniversaries, birthdays, Christmas, or the completion of a big project all are times you can show appreciation and support. Let's say the church has just finished a huge building project that has been time-consuming for your pastor. What an appropriate time to recognize the sacrifice his wife has made and openly demonstrate it by your words and a gift for either her or both of them. One time Glen and Nancy were given a cruise for their wedding anniversary. How that ministered to them both physically and emotionally, knowing what a sacrifice that was for those giving the gift.

Food. Invite the pastor and his entire family over for dinner (but be sensitive not to overdo this one and rob them of time alone as a family), or to give the couple a gift certificate to a nice restaurant and have the children looked after by a member. It may seem like a small thing, but even cheesecake can qualify if that is your favorite food. Sometimes just the fact that someone even knows your wife likes a certain thing and then supplies it can be a show of support. It shows that the member cared enough to give her something she really liked instead of the usual perfume sets, handkerchiefs, or kitchen items.

Child care. Baby-sitting support is always a great help when the minister and his wife need to shop together, such as for Christmas or other times. You can also give them a "coupon" for a free baby-sitting weekend; the kids join various families so the pastor and his wife can have an extended time alone. May we also suggest that at least one to four times a year you provide for them to get away to a motel, to take time together and with the Lord for planning and recharging their marital batteries.

Cash Gifts and Certificates. For both of us and our wives, the thoughtful monetary love gift once a year that we received earlier in our ministries was always so appreciated because of tight finances. Folks, it's hard for pastors and their wives to have their children be dressed in clothes that don't quite match the level of the other children at church or school. When you can't buy the latest fun game or take them to the amusement park as often as you'd like, these things hurt.

One couple took the pastor's kids to the mall and let them each choose an outfit. You may not have much extra money, but how about giving them each some money or a gift certificate to buy something they couldn't get otherwise? Consider also donating coaching—free music, drama, or cooking lessons—to develop their children's skills. Such giving of support to the pastor's family is sadly rare in today's busy, self-centered society. Please don't misunderstand. This is not about money. It's about creative thoughtfulness.

PROFESSIONAL SUPPORT

Volunteering Your Services

We've often said that it seems some days that a pastor not only needs training in theology, but also in law, social work, management, etc. The pastor does a myriad of things; so anything you can do that will take something off his "plate," or will contribute to his being more efficient, will be a welcome support. Here are six creative ways you and others in your congregation can give professional support.

1. Look for articles in magazines and newspapers that you can clip and give the pastor for resource materials. Ask him periodically what he might need. If he plans out his sermon topics in advance, get the list and ask the Lord to show you resources for them.
2. Volunteer to do some research. Research for sermons is time-consuming and often gets squeezed out by other things. Yet pastors are conscientious and want to do the best possible job. Research helps them feel they have covered any given topic well enough to be able to speak with knowledge about it. Your library or computer can provide interesting facts and illustrations for his messages.
3. If you are a computer whiz, and it is appropriate, show him some of the helpful features of his computer he may not have learned. Most pastors are self-taught on the computer; they

would benefit from your help if they could learn to take advantage of more of a particular program's features.

4. Consider giving him a set time each week or month when you would be available to do whatever he needs. There are always errands pastors run that others could handle. Even if the schedules don't mesh, he still knows you've offered and that will be an encouragement to him.

5. Offer to download at home or at the church any resource materials he has that he just has not had the time to add to his computer files. Both Glenn and Glen have often had certain pertinent articles nearby but could not locate the resource from our stacks of papers that are waiting to be filed or downloaded. Your putting them on the pastor's computer makes them quickly and easily accessible.

6. Offer to counsel in certain areas. Counseling is something the older, wiser believers can do to take things from the pastor's packed schedule. Along these lines, premarital counseling is another area the older believers can handle. It is amazing how much time can be freed by assuming responsibility for these two areas.

Providing Resources

All good pastors love to collect various resources. That is why they love books so much, even if they don't read them at the time they buy them. They don't have time to go to the local library for research. Therefore, whatever outside helps they get for their messages usually come from their own library. Yet, books are expensive and pastors cannot afford to buy all they need, let alone want.

God can use you to fill this need.

1. Give the pastor a gift certificate to the local Christian bookstore.
2. If you are in a position of leadership, or even if you are not, suggest to the ruling body that there be adequate moneys budgeted yearly to cover new purchases. This can be an appropriate amount depending on your size and budget. (Some Bible commentaries are very expensive.) Consider designating any extra moneys at the end of the year to books.

3. Include in the church's library budget plans for books that would be useful to both the pastor and the congregation. This way he can have access to them when he needs to.

4. Enter magazine, periodical, and journal subscriptions in your pastor's name. Be certain to ask him which ones he would like. (Glenn recalls: "Susan and I were on such a limited budget in our first pastorate and my desire and need for books and study materials was so great that I sold plasma to a local blood bank for $15 a week!")

5. Challenge some of the Sunday school classes to consider giving towards pastor's professional library. If finances are limited, several classes could combine their moneys. A book at least every quarter would be certain to touch his heart and let him know he has the support of a broad range of the worshipers.

Helping with Continuing Education

Just as professional and denominational conferences are helpful for his marriage (allowing the pastor and his wife to enjoy a new setting and times together), a number of conferences each year could help with continuing education and spiritual inspiration. We both know how very much attending conferences has helped to shape who we are today as pastors, educators, and conference speakers. The Scriptures talk about iron sharpening iron (Proverbs 27:17). Your pastor will be sharpened by a good conference. Yet your pastor may not have the money or feel he can take the time (or even want to ask the leadership for permission to attend). So encourage your leadership to *offer* sending him to one or more conferences. Budget for it. This shows your support of him and of his ministry.

Along these lines, if you have a nearby seminary or a place he can do continuing education, both he and the church will benefit. Be certain to include the costs of professional development in his package of benefits.

Recently one church in Glenn's community gave their pastor a financial grant to enable him to earn his D.Min. degree. A very supportive layman funded the grant.

If you decide to support your pastor in this way, you might want to consider what one church has done: forming an accountability group around the pastor to keep his feet to the fire in pursuing the degree. This helps him know you expect him to take time to complete his degree and will, in turn, lessen any guilt he might feel in taking time from his normal duties to do this.

SABBATICAL SUPPORT

In the section "Encourage Significant Study and Prayer Time," we noted how churches in England refer to their pastors as having "studies" rather than "offices." Now let's turn to their practice on sabbaticals for their clergy. It is not an option for them. It is required that pastors take periodic sabbaticals. During this time the pastor can use it any way the Lord leads: for study, travel, writing, or even marriage restoration.

American churches who offer sabbaticals will encourage a pastor's professional development. Eugene Peterson took a sabbatical from Christ Our King Presbyterian Church in Bel Air, Maryland, to work on *The Message,* a Bible paraphrase that has blessed the Christian community since its publication. Peterson credits this sabbatical as playing an important part in letting him take uninterrupted, concentrated time to focus on writing at the highest level of his ability. As writers we know that trying to write in the midst of many other responsibilities can lead to a manuscript that does not get as much attention as we would ideally like to give it. Oh, for a sabbatical to write.

Peterson represents an exception, for only a minority of U. S. churches offer sabbaticals to let their pastors develop their writing or other professional skills. Be a groundbreaker in your church; ask the church's ruling board to consider a sabbatical policy for the pastor. The concept of a sabbatical comes from God Himself. Remember the seventh year's rest for the land? That was a type of sabbatical.

A FINAL REMINDER

Of course there are other ways to support your pastor; many have been mentioned in previous chapters. We again recommend reading Wes Roberts' fine book, *Support Your Local Pastor* (NavPress).

One final reminder: Pay your pastor well. As your church plans its annual budget, be careful not to let the pastoral salary fall behind.

In the first place, be certain it really is adequate to cover his needs. The ruling body needs periodically to ask him frankly how he is doing financially. Is there enough for his kids' college education? What about emergencies? Savings? Retirement? Don't let him someday be one of the 50 percent of Americans who retire yearly with a pension below the poverty line. And while some pastors have poor pensions, others have no pensions at all. Your pastor has sacrificed to be in ministry. Make certain his old age is cared for well.

Your support of him financially, physically, and emotionally will bear much fruit in his life and ministry. Remember, "we are God's workmanship, created in Christ Jesus to do good works, which God prepared in advance for us to do" (Ephesians 2:10). Go for it!

notes

Preface

1. David Fisher, *The 21st Century Pastor* (Grand Rapids: Zondervan, 1996), 196.

Chapter 1: The State of the Pastorate

1. Gordon MacDonald, "Dear Church, I Quit," *Christianity Today,* 27 June 1980, 16–19.

2. H. B. London and Neil B. Wiseman, *Pastors at Risk* (Wheaton, Ill.: Victor, 1993), 25.

3. Steve Roll, *Holy Burnout* (Tulsa, Okla.: Virgil Hensley, 1996), 16.

4. Ibid., 16, 17.

5. Ibid., 18.

6. Ibid., 19.

7. Andre Bustanoby, "Why Pastors Drop Out," *Christianity Today,* 7 January 1977, 14–15. The study surveyed United Church of Christ pastors.

8. H. B. London, Jr., and Neil B. Wiseman, *Your Pastor is an Endangered Species* (Wheaton, Ill.: Victor, 1996), 17.

9. David Fisher, *The 21st Century Pastor* (Grand Rapids: Zondervan, 1996), 106.

10. John and Sylvia Ronsvalle, *Behind the Stained Glass Windows* (Grand Rapids: Baker, 1996), 39.

11. Ibid., 17.

Chapter 2: Great Expectations

1. George Barna, *Today's Pastors* (Ventura, Calif.: Regal, 1993), 47.

Chapter 3: Exposing Myths in the Pastorate

1. Dave Branon, *Safe at Home 2* (Chicago: Moody, 1997), 48.

2. Greg Johnson, *Youth,* May 1993, 27–28.

Chapter 4: The Pastor's Role

1. "Quotes and Comments," *The United Church Observer,* September 1992, 48.

2. Frank R. Tillapaugh, *The Church Unleashed* (Glendale, Calif.: Regal, 1982), 76.

3. William F. Arndt, Wilbur F. Gingrich, et al, *Greek-English Lexicon* (Grand Rapids: Zondervan, 1979), 418.

4. John MacArthur, Jr., *The MacArthur New Testament Commentary: Ephesians* (Chicago: Moody, 1986), 152.

5. R. Schippers, "artios," *The International Dictionary of New Testament Theology,* ed. Colin Brown (Grand Rapids: Zondervan, 1978), 3:349–50. *Katartizo* is the verb form of *artios.*

6. Andrew T. Lincoln, *Ephesians,* vol. 42, *The Word Biblical Commentary* (Dallas: Word, 1990), 254.

7. Ibid.

Chapter 5: Preyed on or Prayed for

1. Terry Teykle, *Preyed on or Prayed for* (Lexington, Ky.: Bristol, 1993), 23.

2. Wellington Boone, "The Pastor and Moral Character: The Hope of Glory in You," Promise Keepers Pastor's Conference, 14 February 1996, Georgia Dome, Atlanta, Ga.

3. Woodrow Kroll, *The Vanishing Ministry* (Grand Rapids: Kregel, 1991), 67.

4. David Fisher, *The 21st Century Pastor* (Grand Rapids: Zondervan, 1996), 106.

Chapter 7: Positive Participation

1. Adapted from Christina Feldman and Jack Kornfield, eds., *Stories of the Spirit, Stories of the Heart* (San Francisco: Harper, 1991), 303–305.

Chapter 8: Biblical Teamwork

1. C. Peter Wagner, *Your Spiritual Gifts Can Help Your Church Grow* (Ventura, Calif.: Regal, 1994), 249.

Chapter 9: Following the Leader

1. George Barna, *The Power of Vision* (Ventura, Calif.: Regal, 1992), 106.

2. Craig Brian Larson, "Gaining Respect the Old-Fashioned Way," *Leadership* (Spring 1988): 120–3.

3. Joseph M. Stowell, *Shepherding the Church* (Chicago: Moody, 1997), 11.

Chapter 10: Seven Qualities of an Effective Church

1. James Belasco, *Teaching the Elephant to Dance* (New York: NAL/Dutton Plume, 1991), 17–18.

2. Loren B. Mead, *The Once and Future Church* (Washington, D. C.: The Alban Institute, 1994), 28.

Chapter 11: Pastoral Temptations

1. "1991 Survey of Pastors," Fuller Institute of Church Growth (Pasadena, Calif.), as cited in H. B. London, Jr., and Neil B. Wiseman, *Pastors at Risk* (Wheaton, Ill.: Victor, 1993), 22.

2. Results from an informal survey of pastors and wives by Wayne and Margaret Detzler conducted at their *Foundation for Family Life* seminar, 1 April 1995, in Fort Mill, South Carolina. The findings have not been published.

3. "How Common Is Pastoral Indiscretion?" *Leadership* 9 (Winter 1988): 12.

4. Louis McBurney, "Counseling Christian Workers," in *Resources for Christian Counseling,* Gary R. Collins, gen. ed. (Waco, Tex.: Word, 1986), 154–56.

5. "Is the Pastor's Family Safe at Home?" *Leadership 13* (Fall 1992): 40.

6. Ibid.

7. London and Wiseman, *Pastors at Risk,* 86–88.

8. Glen Martin, *Power House: A Step-by-Step Guide to Building a Church that Prays* (Nashville: Broadman, 1994. Pages 207–209 offer good suggestions on how to pray for your own family. These suggestions can be applied to praying for others too.

9. Wes Roberts directs Life Enrichment, 17053 Hastings Avenue, Parker, CO 80134. Telephone: 303-840-4371.

10. London and Wiseman, *Pastors at Risk,* 113.

11. You can contact the Christian Management Association for their research findings at: P.O. Box 4638, Diamond Bar, CA 91765.

12. *Leadership* 9 (Winter 1988): 12.

13. "Is the Pastor's Family Safe at Home?" *Leadership 13* (Fall 1992): 40. The findings were based on responses from 748 pastors.

14. McBurney, "Counseling Christian Workers" in *Resources for Christian Counseling.*

15. George Barna, *What Americans Believe,* as quoted in London and Wiseman, *Pastors at Risk,* 42.

16. William J. Bennett, *Colorado Springs Gazette,* 28 March 1993, D5; as cited in London and Wiseman, *Pastors at Risk,* 42.

17. London and Wiseman, *Pastors at Risk,* 158.

18. Ibid., 163–64. Each of the four A's is discussed in depth as part of an extended interview with Hart in chapter 8 of *Pastors at Risk,* pages 157–72. We highly recommend this chapter, which includes the interview with Professor Hart and offers pastors suggestions for recognizing and coping with high stress.

19. *Current Thoughts and Trends,* December 1992, as quoted in London and Wiseman, *Pastors at Risk,* 166.

20. London and Wiseman, *Pastors at Risk,* 78–80.

21. C. Peter Wagner in *Ministries Today,* November/December 1992, as quoted in London and Wiseman, *Pastors at Risk,* 179.

Moody Press, a ministry of Moody Bible Institute,
is designed for education, evangelization, and edification.
If we may assist you in knowing more about Christ
and the Christian life, please write us without obligation:
Moody Press, c/o MLM, Chicago, Illinois 60610.